Voice Recognition

For a complete listing of the *Artech House Telecommunications Library*, turn to the back of this book.

Voice Recognition

Richard L. Klevans
Robert D. Rodman

Artech House
Boston • London

Library of Congress Cataloging-in-Publication Data
Klevans, Richard L.
Voice recognition / Richard L. Klevans, Robert D. Rodman.
   p.   cm. — (Artech House telecommunications library)
Includes bibliographical references and index.
ISBN 0-89006-927-1 (alk. paper)
  1. Speech processing systems.   2. Automatic speech recognition.
3. Voiceprints.   4. Natural language processing (Computer science)
I. Rodman, Robert D. II. Title. III. Series.
TK7882.S65K55   1997
006.4'54—dc21   97-30792
                                                                                                                                                                  CIP

British Library Cataloguing in Publication Data
Klevans, Richard L.
  Voice recognition
  1. Automatic speech recognition
  I. Title. II. Rodman, Robert D.
  006.4'54

  ISBN 0-89006-927-1

Cover design by Jennifer L. Stuart

© 1997 ARTECH HOUSE, INC.
685 Canton Street
Norwood, MA 02062

  All rights reserved. Printed and bound in the United States of America. No part of this book may be reproduced or utilized in any form or by any means, electronic or mechanical, including photocopying, recording, or by any information storage and retrieval system, without permission in writing from the publisher.
  All terms mentioned in this book that are known to be trademarks or service marks have been appropriately capitalized. Artech House cannot attest to the accuracy of this information. Use of a term in this book should not be regarded as affecting the validity of any trademark or service mark.

International Standard Book Number: 0-89006-927-1
Library of Congress Catalog Card Number: 97-30792

10 9 8 7 6 5 4 3 2 1

Contents

Chapter 1 Introduction	1
Speech Synthesis	1
Speech Recognition	3
Speaker Classification	4
Areas of Application for Voice Recognition	6
Design Tradeoffs in Voice Recognition	7
Text-Dependent Versus Text-Independent	7
Ideal Recording Environment Versus Noisy Environment	8
Speaker Verification Versus Speaker Identification	9
Real-Time Operation Versus Off-Line Operation	9
Regarding This Book	10
Intended Readers	10
What Is Covered	11
Why?	12
References	13
Chapter 2 Background of Voice Recognition	15
Voiceprint Analysis	16
Parameter Extraction	20
The Parameter Extraction Process	20
Types of Parameters	21
Evaluation of Parameters	27
Distance Measures	29
Pattern Recognition	32

Voice Recognition in Noisy Environments 54
Summary 56
References 57

Chapter 3 Methods of Context-Free Voice
           Recognition 61
Voice Recognition in Law Enforcement 61
    Forensic Recognition Classification 62
Ideal Voice Recognition 64
A Segregating Voice-Recognition System 72
    System Tasks 75
    Channel Variation Compensation 94
    Software Implementation 99
Logistics of Forensic Speaker Identification 101
Summary 105
References 105

Chapter 4 Experimental Results 107
Test Utterance Length Experiments 107
Large Population Results 112
Filtered Data Test 114
Channel Compensation Tests 116
    Average Filter Compensation Technique
    Experiment 117
    Rehumanizing Filter Technique
    Experiment 119
Secondary Parameters 121
    Secondary Parameter Usage 130
    Effects of Varying the Cutoff Value 131
    Best-Case Secondary Parameter Usage 132
Mock Forensic Cases 135
    SBI Case 1 136
    SBI Case 2 144
    SBI Case 3 147
Summary 148
References 149

Chapter 5   The Future of Context-Free Voice
            Recognition   151
         Rehumanizing Filter Technique Tests   151
         Voice-Recognition Databases   153
         Medium-Term Goals   156
         Long-Term Goals   157
         Other Applications   158
         Summary   159
         References   160

Chapter 6   Conclusions   161

About the Authors   165

Index   167

Introduction 1

Speech processing by computer is a major field of endeavor. It is multidisciplinary, encompassing electrical engineering, computer science, and linguistics. Its applications affect nearly every discipline imaginable—from art, in which presentations may be enhanced by programs that permit figures to lip-synch speech, to zoology, in which animated, speaking agents explain animal physiology on a computer screen. The effects of speech processing are pervasive in daily life and are especially prevalent in such industries as transportation, telephone communications, and computer operations.

There are three distinct subfields of speech processing, which, for the most part, are independent of one another. These are *speech synthesis, speech recognition,* and *speaker classification.*

SPEECH SYNTHESIS

Speech synthesis has ancient historical roots. Attempts to artificially produce the human voice date back at least to the 18th century. In 1779, Christian Gottlieb Kratzenstein constructed a set of acoustic resonators whose design was based on the *vox humana* pipes of the organ. The resonators simulated the shapes of the mouth when the various vowels, a, e, i, o, and u were pronounced. For this innovation,

Kratzenstein won a prize from the Imperial Academy of St. Petersburg.

In 1791 a Viennese engineer, Wolfgang von Kempelen, built an improved model. His resonators had bellows to replicate the pulmonary airstream and other structures to simulate the different parts of the vocal tract. Alexander Graham Bell saw a replica of the device in Edinburgh and was so impressed that he attempted to construct a "talking-head" version. This early speech synthesizer was cast from a human skull and used various materials for articulatory organs such as the tongue, lips and teeth. The vocal cords were simulated with rubber bands, and the whole device was powered by bellows. The machine could produce vowel and nasal sounds.

With the advent of the electronic age, it was no longer necessary to build actual physical models of the human vocal tract. Speech sounds could be replicated electronically. Of course, this was easier said than done. A much deeper understanding of speech acoustics led to the first *vocoder* (from *voice coder*), an early version of which was displayed at the 1939 World's Fair in New York. Significant improvements took place over the next 30 years, principally at AT&T Bell Laboratories, where scientists were interested in the low bandwidth rates of voice transmission that could be achieved with synthetic speech.

The invention of the integrated circuit, allowing computationally intense algorithms to be run on a digital computer, led to the first formant synthesizers, the forerunners of the modern, digitally based speech synthesizer. Today, speech synthesizers are nearly as intelligible as the human voice. There is still a distinct lack of naturalness, a "machine accent." Much of the research in the past few years has focused on improving the text-to-speech algorithms that allow speech synthesizers to voice the written word and to give voice and sense to tabular data such as weather statistics. Many challenges have been overcome, but several remain. The most difficult of these is achieving natural-sounding prosodics, which encompasses the correct placement of both word- and phrase-level stress, correct word pitch and sentence intonation, and segment durations that are correctly apportioned within the word.

SPEECH RECOGNITION

The goal of speech recognition is the converse of speech synthesis: to transliterate speech into written form. The task is similar to that of the court stenographer, who transcribes all speech occurring in the courtroom onto the printed page.

History again looks back to the giant figure of Alexander Graham Bell. He had an abiding interest in speech for the deaf and wanted to build a device that would make speech visible. But although he invented his own phonetic alphabet, his dream of speech recognition—the transcription of speech into the alphabetic symbols—was never achieved. His "failure" was instructive, however, and he ended up inventing the telephone.

Real progress had to wait until the 1950s, when once again, AT&T Bell Labs was at the forefront. AT&T scientists built the first speech recognizer, a machine capable of recognizing the English digits zero through nine. The device used a simple pattern-recognition scheme. Reference templates for each digit would be collected from a particular speaker and later compared with that same speaker's individual utterances.

Successive systems improved the scheme through dynamic time warping, which compensated for variable utterance length—so that "good morning," for example, could be successfully matched with "gooooooooood mooooooorrrrning." With the increase in computational power of the 1980s and 1990s, statistical methods involving so-called hidden Markov models (HMMs) and neural nets led to further improvements.

The most favorable conditions for robust speech recognition occur when ... words ... are ... spoken ... in ... isolation, when the same speaker both trains and uses the system, and when the surrounding environment is free of background noise. The goal of speech scientists, however, is for a machine to recognize "naturallysmoothflowingspeech," from persons unknown to the machine, under the realistic noisy conditions of everyday living—the same conditions under which people ordinarily communicate.

SPEAKER CLASSIFICATION

Speaker classification refers to the process of extracting information about an individual from their speech. This is a fascinating area of research. From speech alone, fairly accurate guesses can be made as to whether the speaker is male or female, adult or child. A person's mood, emotional state, and attitude may be indicated in their speech. Anger, fear, belligerence, sadness, indignation, reluctance, or elation may all be detectable in the speech signal.

Automatic language identification—that is, the process of identifying what language a person is speaking, whether he or she is speaking formally or informally, to intimates or to strangers, to persons of higher or lower social rank, to children or to adults, to foreigners or to nationals—may be derived from the speech signal. Evidence of an individual's nationality, region of upbringing, social standing, and education level leaves traces in their speech.

If it is not known in advance whether one or more persons is speaking, this may be determined by analyzing the speech signal. A highly specialized subarea is *speaker separation*, a process that attempts to isolate individual voices. This process of focusing exclusively on one speaker's voice among many others in the vicinity is also known as the "cocktail party effect."

An accurate, real-time portrayal of the speaker's lips, tongue, mouth, and jaw during speech utterance may be derived from the speech signal without the necessity of speech-recognition or electromechanical devices attached to the jaw. This is the basis for the subfield of *lip-synching*. Finally, the most heavily investigated subarea of speaker classification is *voice recognition*, often called *speaker recognition*,[1] the subject of this monograph. This may be thought of as the "Hi, it's me" phenomenon, in which one trusts to voice recognition that the person addressed will know who "me" is.

Voice recognition is complementary to speech recognition. Both techniques use similar methods of speech signal processing up to a point, but speech recognition, if it is to be speaker-independent, must purposefully ignore any idiosyncratic speech characteristics of the speaker and focus on those aspects of the speech signal richest in linguistic information. Conversely, voice recognition must amplify those idiosyncratic speech characteristics that individuate a person and suppress linguistic characteristics, which have no bearing on the recognition of the individual speaker.

Humans are fairly adept at speaker recognition. A human can easily determine the identity of familiar speakers on the telephone after listening to only a short segment of speech. Humans are less effective at recognizing the voices of unfamiliar speakers. However, they can be "trained" through the process of becoming familiar with a given speaker and their speech. Designers of voice-recognition systems try to duplicate roughly the processes humans use to recognize speakers. Such systems must be trained to know how a given person "sounds," and the more training data, the better, just as the better you know a person, the more likely you are to recognize him or her by voice alone.

The range of sounds that may be produced by a human being is related to the physical size and shape of the speaker's

---

1. We will use these terms interchangeably for stylistic variety.

vocal tract [1]. The vocal tract consists of the glottis, tongue, velum or soft palate, hard palate, teeth, nasal cavity, and lips. The elasticity of the tissue in the vocal tract also affects the sounds produced by an individual. Because there are so many physical parameters contributing to the range of sounds that each individual can make, we believe that an individual may be uniquely identified by voice alone. This is the underlying thesis of our approach to voice recognition.

AREAS OF APPLICATION FOR VOICE RECOGNITION

The ability to identify people uniquely by their voices alone leads to several application areas. To date, voice-recognition technology has had greatest impact in the area of security. While access to secured areas may be restricted by means of keys, magnetic cards, and lock combinations, such devices are fallible because they can be easily stolen. Voice recognition can provide an alternative, more secure means of permitting entry.

Of course, although voices cannot be stolen, they can be copied with recording devices. Voice-based security systems must protect themselves against this ploy. One way to do this is by varying the text to be spoken by the person wishing access, which would require the combination of voice recognition and speech recognition. In such a case, both the identity and the linguistic content of the speech must be verified.

Another ongoing security concern is that of access to computer systems via terminals, phone lines, or automatic teller machines. Currently, such access is typically restricted by the use of passwords or personal identification numbers. But again, such codes can be lost, stolen, or copied. As with physical-access situations, voice recognition could provide increased security for computer systems.

The use of voice recognition in law enforcement is becoming commonplace in cases where voice-recordings of suspects form part of the evidence [2]. Such cases might include bomb threats, ransom negotiations, undercover tape recordings, or wiretaps. Results are not always definitive, but they can often direct the investigation away from unlikely suspects and toward more likely ones. The results of voice-recognition analysis are not yet freely admitted as evidence in the courtroom, but with improved techniques, and with judges now beginning to understand the significance of probabilistic findings, we expect the situation to change in the future.

In combination with other technologies, further areas of application for voice recognition include aids for the hearing-disabled (Alexander Graham Bell would be pleased), spoken-dialogue systems, learning technologies, virtual conferencing, and virtual impersonation.

DESIGN TRADEOFFS IN VOICE RECOGNITION

The design of a voice recognition system can be greatly affected by the targeted application area of the system. Many tradeoffs are necessary to build a system that meets the constraints of the application. Some of the most common tradeoffs are listed below.

Text-Dependent Versus Text-Independent

Text-dependent voice recognition systems may be trained by having each speaker read a prescribed text. During the recognition (testing) phase, unknown speakers must speak the same prescribed text that was used for training. Text-dependent systems usually require each speaker to read the prescribed text only a few times during training. These systems are suitable for security applications in which the valid speakers are cooperative.

Text-independent systems allow the user to read any text during both training and testing. Typical text-independent systems require more training data than text-dependent systems. This is necessary to ensure that the speaker's full range of vocal sounds are captured during training. Text-independent systems are suitable for applications in which the speakers are not cooperative—such as in law enforcement, where investigators cannot force a suspect to speak a prescribed text.[2]

Text-dependent systems can be implemented in a manner similar to discrete-word speech-recognition systems. However, instead of a system that returns the name of the stored word template that most closely matches the word spoken, the speaker-recognition system would return the name of the individual whose template for the prescribed text most closely matched the speech of the unknown speaker. Text-independent systems are more difficult to build and cannot use this simple technique.

Ideal Recording Environment Versus Noisy Environment

Ideal recording environments consist of high-quality microphones used in rooms with little or no background noise and reverberation. In an ideal recording environment, the same microphone and room is used for both training and testing sessions. Using the same equipment for both training and testing eliminates any channel variations that might be falsely used as characteristics for identification.

Unfortunately, many practical uses of voice recognition necessarily occur in noisy environments and in situations in which channel variation is inevitable. A bomb threat recorded by a 911 logging device, a surveillance tape of a drug deal, a

---

2. A court order may be obtained obliging a suspect to repeat a fixed phrase. However, noncooperation can take many subtle forms, such as drawing out or clipping words, shifting stress, altering intonation, or interjecting coughs or other nonlinguistic sounds that will confound the process.

wiretap, or a personal threat on a home answering-machine all engender noise and channel variation. Much of today's research in voice recognition addresses the issues raised by noisy environments and idiosyncratic channel usage.

Speaker Verification Versus Speaker Identification

Speaker verification means determining whether a speaker is the person they claim to be—for example, to gain entry to a secure area. Verification systems must deal with two kinds of errors: false rejection and false approval. False rejection occurs when a legitimate person is denied access to the secure area; false approval occurs when an impostor is allowed to enter the secure area. The designers of speaker-verification systems must adjust the decision criteria so that false approval will be as low as possible without causing the false rejection rate to become too high.

Speaker identification is the process of determining which speaker in a group of known speakers most closely matches the unknown speaker. The identification may be *closed set*, in which it is known a priori that the unknown is in the set of speakers, or *open set*, in which the unknown speaker may or may not be a member of the set of known speakers. For closed-set identification, the voice recognition system can simply choose the known speaker who most closely matches the unknown, providing there are no close runner-ups. Open-set identification is more difficult. It is equivalent to performing a closed-set identification followed by verification. The verification task is needed to determine if the match between the unknown and the "winner" of the identification task are close enough to be the same speaker.

Real-Time Operation Versus Off-Line Operation

The nature of security applications requires that the voice recognition system respond within a short period of time.

Other applications, such as those related to law enforcement, may not have this constraint.

REGARDING THIS BOOK

Newspaper reporters are customarily urged to learn their "wh-" words—"who," "what," and "why"—and though neither of us is a reporter, we shall follow their lead in describing our book.

Intended Readers

This is a book about getting computers to recognize people by voice. It is written for professionals and consumers of voice recognition in the areas described below.

Speech Processing

In the field of speech processing, this book will be of interest to technical managers and their staffs, engineers, computer scientists, speech scientists, and human-factors professionals.

Security

The book is suitable for security officers of businesses in which security is vital, such as banks, hotels, pharmaceutical corporations, and arms manufacturers. Technically oriented homeowners concerned about voice-activated home-security systems will also find the book of interest.

Law Enforcement

Recent years have seen an increase in bomb threats (witness the hundreds of examples at the 1996 Olympic Games) and similar cases in which the voice of a threatening caller is recorded, and nowadays, much work in law enforcement relies on recorded voices from surveillance or wiretapping activities. To this extent, appropriately trained employees of the Federal Bureau of Investigation, the State Bureaus of Investigation, the Central Intelligence Agency, the National Security Agency, and police and sheriff departments throughout the country will find this book relevant to their needs.

Justice

In the near future, judges, prosecutors, and defense attorneys are likely to encounter evidence obtained from voice recognition systems. A technical understanding of this field will be necessary to discuss intelligently the admission of such evidence and the weight that should be attributed to it.

Education and Training

The book is suitable for university professors, lecturers, and students as supplementary reading in courses in speech processing, speech communications, and signal processing. (Such courses are now offered not only on college and university campuses but through the National Technical University via the Internet and at such companies as IBM, Bell Northern Research, and AT&T, to name a few.)

Research in Voice Recognition

Because this book is an adapted scholarly work, it will be required reading for researchers in both the industrial and academic milieus who wish to pursue voice recognition beyond the leading edge.

What Is Covered

This book provides a general discussion of computer voice recognition systems, including the following:

- The basic underlying concepts;
- A comparison with voice recognition by the human being;
- What are the significant application areas;
- The fundamental design tradeoffs;
- A summary of the previous research in all areas of voice recognition;
- A presentation of our multigranular segregating system for context-free voice recognition, which includes justification for the design strategy and a careful explanation of the details of system implementation, the results of experiments carried out using the system, and examples of actual cases;
- Considerations of how to normalize for channel variance and an outline of other areas within the field in which future research is needed;
- The conclusions drawn from this work.

Why?

We are a linguist and a computer scientist collaborating on research in the area of speech processing. In the major areas of speech recognition and speech synthesis, much of the basic research has been done, and what remains is being carried out by well-established groups such as those at Carnegie-Mellon University and Bell Labs.

Several years ago, we decided to tackle the problem of automatic language identification. In doing this research, we discovered, more or less serendipitously, methods that worked extremely well in text-independent (which we also call *context-free*) speaker identification. So we switched areas. It was not as dramatic as Democrats becoming Republicans or vice versa. The research methods are quite similar. We kept the same friends and colleagues. We used the same basic hardware and software. Only the goals changed.

We found tremendous general interest in our research. Besides our collaboration with law-enforcement officials, we had calls from defense lawyers in drug cases, a torts lawyer in a case regarding a pornographic videotape, and a cartoon historian trying to figure out if Walt Disney had provided the voice of Ferdinand the Bull's mother in one of Disney's earlier cartoon films.

In carrying out research in voice recognition, we found relatively little literature in the text-independent subarea, and much of what we did find consisted of highly technical fragments of research published in journals and conference proceedings to which most people do not have access.

This book is intended to provide a comprehensive overview of voice recognition, and in that context we present our own original findings in the special area of text-independent voice recognition.

References

[1] Rabiner, Lawrence R., and Schafer, Ronald W., *Digital Processing of Speech Signal*, Englewood Cliffs, New Jersey: Prentice-Hall, Inc., 1978.

[2] Bolt, Richard H., et al., "Identification of a Speaker by Speech Spectrograms," *Science*, Vol. 166, Oct. 1969.

Background of Voice Recognition 2

This chapter will present a review of the research in the area of voice recognition. Initially, research in this area concentrated on determining whether speakers' voices were unique or at least distinguishable from those of a group of other speakers. In these studies, manual intervention was necessary to carry out the recognition task. As computer power increased and knowledge about speech signals improved, research became aimed at fully automated systems executed on general-purpose computers or specially designed computer hardware.

Voice recognition consists of two major tasks: *feature extraction* and *pattern recognition*. Feature extraction attempts to discover characteristics of the speech signal unique to the individual speaker. The process is analogous to a police description of a suspect, which typically lists height, weight, skin color, facial shape, body type, and any distinguishing marks or disfigurements. Pattern recognition refers to the matching of features in such a way as to determine, within probabilistic limits, whether two sets of features are from the same or different individuals. In this chapter, we will discuss research related to these tasks. The chapter will conclude with a short description of methods for dealing with noise in voice-recognition systems.

VOICEPRINT ANALYSIS

The first type of automatic speaker recognition, called *voiceprint analysis*, was begun in the 1960s. The term *voiceprint* was derived from the more familiar term *fingerprint*. Researchers hoped that voiceprints would provide a reliable method for uniquely identifying people by their voices, just as fingerprints had proven to be a reliable method of identification in forensic situations.

Voiceprint analysis was only a semiautomatic process. First, a graphical representation of each speaker's voice was created. Then, human experts manually determined whether two graphs represented utterances spoken by the same person. The graphical representations took one of two forms: a *speech spectrogram* (called a *bar voiceprint* at the time)—see Figure 2.1—or a contour voiceprint [1]. The former, the more commonly used form, consists of a representation of a spoken utterance in which time is displayed on the abscissa, frequency on the ordinate, and spectral energy as the darkness at a given point.

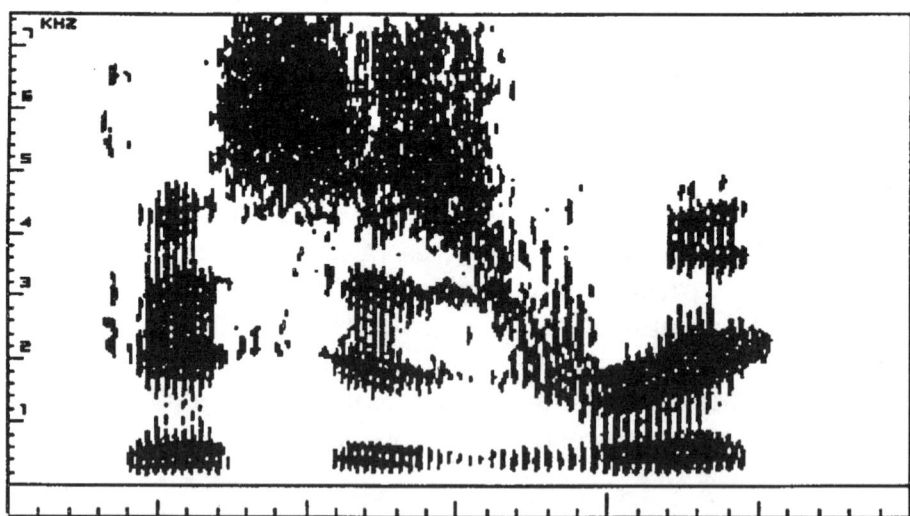

Figure 2.1 Spectrogram of author saying, "This is Rick."

Prior to a voiceprint identification attempt, spectrograms would have been produced by a *sound spectrograph* from recordings of the speakers in question. Typically, the input data for voiceprint analysis consisted of recordings of utterances of 10 commonly used words—such as "the," "you," and "I"—from each speaker in the set to be identified. These 10 words can be thought of as roughly analogous to the 10 fingers used in fingerprint analysis. Human experts determined the identity of speakers by visually inspecting the spectrograms of a given word spoken by several known speakers and comparing those to a spectrogram of the same word spoken by an unknown speaker.

The experts looked for features of the spectrograms that best characterized each speaker. Some commonly used features were absolute formant frequency, formant bandwidths, and formant trajectories. Formants are bands of energy in the spectrogram that are related to the resonant frequencies of the speaker's vocal tract. Therefore, formant locations and trajectories are related to the fixed shapes of the speaker's vocal tract as well as the way in which the speaker manipulates his or her vocal tract during utterances.

The voiceprint identification method described above had many flaws. First, identification was based on the subjective judgment of human experts. Second, multiple voiceprints of a word spoken by one person can vary as much as voiceprints by two different speakers speaking the same word. This phenomenon introduces the general problem of interspeaker versus intraspeaker variance that is of primary concern for all voice-recognition research. A final concern was the vulnerability of the voiceprint identification process to impostors that had been trained to mimic other speakers. Thus, researchers were uncertain about the worth of voiceprint identification. In the 1960s, a number of experiments were performed that addressed these issues. L.G. Kersta reported an error rate of 1% for 2000 identification attempts with populations of 9 to 15 known speakers for each unknown [1]. Richard Bolt summarized the results of several similar studies with widely varying error rates [2]. Some studies reported error rates as high as 21% and others as low as 0.42%. Bolt criticized all the studies as being artificial inasmuch as the experiments consisted of matching tasks. If used as evidence in court, he pointed out, the analysis would be a verification task, in which the experts would have to decide from two sets of voiceprints (one set from the accused, one set from the unknown) whether or not the accused and the unknown person were the same.

The inconsistent experimental evidence caused experts to disagree about the viability of voiceprints. Kersta's original study led him to believe that voiceprint analysis could be as effective as fingerprint analysis:

> Other experimental data encourages me to believe that unique identifications from voiceprints can be made. Work continues, there being questions to answer and problems to solve.... It is my opinion, however, that identifiable uniqueness does exist in each voice, and that masking, disguising, or distorting the voice will not defeat identification if the speech is intelligible [1].

A study by Richard Bolt and others a few years later reached the opposite conclusion:

> Fingerprints show directly the physical pattern of the finger producing them, and these patterns are readily discernible. Spectrographic patterns and the sound waves that they represent are not, however, related so simply and directly to vocal anatomy; moreover, the spectrogram is not the primary evidence, but only a graphic means for examining the sounds that a speaker makes [2].

Between 1970 and 1985, the Federal Bureau of Investigation (FBI) made extensive use of spectrogram identification, the results of which were analyzed by Bruce Koenig [3]. The FBI formulated a 10-point procedural protocol dictating how voice comparison was to take place. The Bureau insisted on high-quality recordings, from which spectrograms in the frequency range of 0–4,000 Hz were to be made. FBI technicians examined twenty words pronounced alike (supposedly) for similarities and differences, and these results were supplemented by aural comparisons made by repeatedly and simultaneously playing the two voice samples on separate tape recorders. In the end, the examiner determined whether two exemplars were "no or low confidence," "very similar," or "very dissimilar," and these results were confirmed by two other examiners. Identification of an individual was only claimed in the presence of a sufficiently high percentage of "very similar" determinations.

A survey of the results of 2,000 voice comparisons found that in two-thirds (1,304) of the cases, examiners had no or low confidence; in 318 cases there was a positive identification; and in 378 cases a positive elimination. There was one false identification and two false eliminations. Koenig observes:

> Most of the no or low confidence decisions were due to poor recording quality and/or an insufficient number of comparable words. Decisions were also affected by high-pitched voices (usually female) and some forms of voice disguise [3].

The attempt to use voiceprints in a forensic setting left unanswered many questions about the practicality of using voice to identify individuals uniquely. It became clear that research must be focused on the following goals:

1. Automating the recognition procedures;
2. Freeing recognition procedures from dependency on fixed words;
3. Standardizing testing so improvements in procedures could be measured;
4. Handling noisy signals;
5. Coping with unknown and/or inadequate channels;
6. Dealing with intervoice and intravoice variation both natural and artificial (i.e., disguised voice).

Advances in digital computer hardware in the mid 1980s made achievement of these goals seem possible. The six points enumerated above were the basis of many research programs in voice recognition during subsequent years. These programs will be discussed in the remaining sections of this chapter. Since voice-recognition research progressed along many different paths after the 1960s, a historical perspective is not fully appropriate. Thus, we have partitioned the discussion of research by task: *parameter extraction, distance measurements, pattern recognition techniques*, and *special considerations*.

PARAMETER EXTRACTION

In this section, we will discuss methods of extracting information from speech waveforms. Parameter or feature extraction consists of preprocessing an electrical signal to transform it into a usable digital form, applying algorithms to extract only speaker-related information from the signal, and determining the quality of the extracted parameters.

The Parameter Extraction Process

The preprocessing required by voice-recognition systems uses digital signal processing (DSP) methods that are common to all computer speech systems. First, the sound wave created by an individual's speech is transduced into an analog electrical signal via a microphone. The electrical signal is sampled and quantized, resulting in a digital representation of the analog signal. Typical representations of signals for voice-recognition systems are sampled at rates of between 8 and 16 kHz with 8 to 16 bits of resolution [4].

The digital signal may then be subjected to conditioning. For example, bandpass filtering can be used for attenuating parts of the spectrum that are corrupted with additive noise. Spectral flattening can be used to improve the pitch extraction process by compensating for the effect of the vocal tract on the excitation signal created by the vibrating vocal folds. Many other conditioning techniques have been reported. After the signal has been conditioned, it may then be used as input to an algorithm for parameter extraction (Figure 2.2).

Types of Parameters

The most basic type of parameters used for voice recognition are either quantifiable by a human listener, such as pitch or

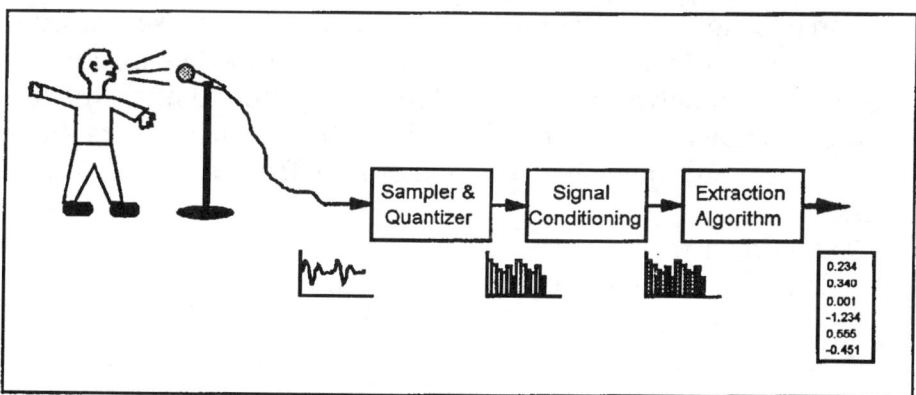

Figure 2.2 The parameter extraction process.

loudness, or have been borrowed from systems for speech coding, recognition, or synthesis.

Pitch

The pitch of a speaker's voice during an utterance is roughly describable by a human listener. The human listener can sense the average pitch and detect changes of pitch during an utterance. Although it is not an easy process, pitch determination can be performed by computer algorithms. Many different algorithms have been devised for pitch extraction [5].

At first glance, pitch appears to be a valuable parameter for speaker identification. For example, a distinction between male voices, female voices, and juvenile voices can be made based mainly on pitch. However, pitch is affected by the speaker's mood and can be modified intentionally by an uncooperative speaker or one with criminal intent.

Frequency Representations

A second simple type of parameter is the frequency representation of a signal in various time frames. This representation is equivalent to a spectrogram in numerical form. The numerical form of a spectrogram is usually computed using the fast Fourier transform (FFT) algorithm. Many processors have been designed specifically to execute FFT algorithms in real time.

The results obtainable using the FFT algorithm vary with the design parameters of the algorithm. If short analysis windows are used, the FFT algorithm accurately represents changes in the spectral energy of the signal over time but will not have high resolution in the frequency dimension. Conversely, if long analysis windows are used, the results will be accurate in the frequency dimension but coarse in the time dimension.[1] Most voice-processing systems use FFTs with moderate-sized analysis windows (approximately 20 ms). The magnitudes of the resulting FFT coefficients are commonly called inverse filter spectral coefficients.

As mentioned earlier, formant frequencies, which can be determined from the frequency representation of a speech signal, are related to the resonant cavities of an individual's vocal tract. Thus, researchers believed that this correlation might be useful for voice recognition. The original research in this area required manual intervention for determining formant frequencies, but soon, automated methods became available [6].

LPC Coefficients

Linear predictive coding (LPC) coefficients are commonly used as features for voice-recognition systems. LPC was developed as an efficient method for representing speech signals and became widely used in many areas of speech processing [7].

In LPC, a parametric representation of speech is created by using past values of the signal to predict future values. The nth value of the speech signal can be predicted by the formula below:

$$\hat{s}_n = \sum_{i=1}^{p} s_{n-i} a_i$$

where s_n is the nth speech sample, the a_k are the predictor coefficients, and $\hat{s}_n$ is the prediction of the nth value of the

---

1. This is actually a manifestation of a classical trade-off in physics known as the Heisenberg Uncertainty Principle. Most readers will know it as follows: "one cannot determine both the position and the velocity of an elementary particle with complete accuracy; the more highly determined the one, the less highly determined the other." It is a consequence of the wave description of matter and, in the particular case of digital signal processing, of the wave description of sound.

speech signal. Predictor coefficients can be estimated by an iterative algorithm that minimizes the mean square error between the predicted waveform, $\hat{s}$, and the actual waveform, s. The number of coefficients derived using LPC, p, is a parameter of the algorithm and is roughly related to the number of real and complex poles of the vocal tract filter. With more coefficients, the original signal can be reconstructed more accurately but at a higher computational cost. Typically, 12 coefficients are calculated for speech sampled at 10 kHz [8–10].

Although the LPC predictor coefficients can be used directly as features, many transformations of the coefficients are also used. The transformations are designed to create a new set of coefficients that are optimized for various performance criteria.

The most commonly used transformation is that which derives the anagrammatically named *cepstrum* from the spectrum. The LPC-derived *cepstral* coefficients are defined as follows, where c_i is the ith cepstral coefficient:

$$c_1 = a_1$$

$$c_i = a_i + \sum_{k=1}^{i-1} ((1 - (k/i))a_k c_{i-k}), \ 1 < i \leq p$$

Unlike LPC coefficients, cepstral coefficients are independent and the distance between cepstral coefficient vectors can be calculated with a Euclidean-type distance measure [11].

The reflection coefficients are natural byproducts of the computation of the LPC predictor coefficients. They are defined from the following backward recursion:

$$k_i = b_{i,i}$$

$$b_{j,i-1} = \frac{b_{j,i} + b_{i,i}b_{i-j,i}}{1 - k_i^2}$$

$$b_{j,p} = a_j$$
$$1 \leq j \leq i - 1, \ 1 \leq i \leq p$$

where k_i is the value of ith reflection coefficient, $i = (p, p - 1, \ldots, 1)$, a_i is the ith LPC coefficient, $b_{j,i}$ is a variable within the recurrence relation, and p is the number of LPC coefficients.

The log area coefficients are defined by:

$$g_i = \log\left(\frac{1 - k_i}{1 + k_i}\right) \ 1 \leq i \leq p$$

where g_i is the ith log area coefficient, k_i is the ith reflection coefficient and $k_i \leq 1$ [12].

Another such transformation is the impulse response function, calculated as follows:

$$h_i = \sum_{k=1}^{p} a_k, h_{1-k} \quad i > 0$$
$$h_i = 1 \quad i = 0$$
$$h_i = 0 \quad i < 0$$

where a_k is the kth LPC coefficient and p is equal to the number of LPC coefficients. The impulse response function is the time-domain output function that would result from inputting an impulse function to a finite duration impulse response (FIR) filter that used the LPC coefficients as the filter coefficients.

Other Parameters

The selection of features, for the most part, is not affected by the type of application. Most text-independent voice-recognition systems currently developed have used the same kinds of features as are used in text-dependent systems. However, some features have been developed specifically to improve performance in noisy environments.

For example, Delta-Cepstrum coefficients are calculated by determining the differences between cepstral coefficients in each time frame. Thus, any constant bias caused by the channel would be removed [11]. The relative spectral-based coefficients (RASTA) use a series of transformations to remove linear distortion of a signal (i.e., filtering). With this technique, the slow-moving variations in the frequency domain are detected and removed. Fast-moving variations—caused by the speech itself—are captured in the resulting parameters [13,14]. The intensity deviation spectrum (IDS) parameters constitute another attempt to remove the frequency characteristics of the transmission channel by normalizing by the mean value at each frequency in the spectrum [15].

Other miscellaneous features have also been suggested: perceptual linear predictive (PLP) coefficients attempt to modify LPC coefficients based on the way human perception and physiology effects sounds [16]. Line spectral pair (LSP) frequencies have also been used as parameters. LSP frequencies are derived from the LPC coefficients and have a rough correlation to formant bandwidths and locations [17]. The partial correlation (PARCOR) coefficients, which are another natural byproduct of LPC analysis, have also been used [18]. Finally, smoothed discrete Wigner distributions (SDWD) attempt to eliminate the problem of time versus frequency accuracy when calculating FFTs. By smoothing the FFT calculation in an efficient manner, the resulting SDWD parameters achieve accuracy in both time and frequency dimensions without a high computation cost. The resulting parameters have been used effectively for voice recognition [19].

The list of features used for voice recognition discussed in this section consists of many parameters that are common to other voice-processing applications as well as some parameters that were devised specifically for the voice-recognition task. Most of these parameters were derived by performing some kind of transformation of the LPC coefficients.

Evaluation of Parameters

To build a successful voice-recognition system, one must make informed decisions concerning which parameters to use. The penalties for choosing parameters incorrectly include poor recognition performance and excessive processing time and storage space. The goal of parameter evaluation should be to determine the smallest set of parameters which contain as much useful information as possible.

The theory of analysis of variance provides a method for determining the relative merits of parameters for voice recognition. Features are identified which remain relatively constant for the speech of a single individual but vary over the speech of different individuals. Typical voice-recognition systems use a set of parameters (features) that may be represented by a vector **W**:

$$\mathbf{W} = [w_1, w_2, \ldots, w_p]$$

where w_1, w_2, etc., are individual features such as LPC coefficients or cepstral coefficients. Numerous vectors can be obtained by performing feature extraction on evenly spaced analysis windows throughout utterances spoken by the individuals to be recognized. Thus, at different time positions in an utterance, the same parameters are calculated.

The F-ratio for each feature, k, in **W** can be determined as follows [6]:

$$F_k = \frac{\text{(Variance of Speaker Means)}}{\text{(Average Within Speaker Variance)}} \qquad (2.1)$$

If s vectors have been collected for each of q number of speakers, then:

$$F_k = \frac{\frac{s}{q-1} \sum_{i=1}^{q} (S_{i,k} - U_k)^2}{\frac{1}{(s-1)} \sum_{i=1}^{q} \sum_{j=1}^{s} (w_{i,j,k} - S_{i,k})^2} \quad (2.2)$$

$$S_{i,k} = \frac{1}{s} \sum_{j=1}^{s} w_{i,j,k} \quad (2.3)$$

$$U_k = \frac{1}{q} \sum_{i=1}^{q} S_{i,k} \quad (2.4)$$

where $w_{i,j,k}$ is the value of the kth feature for the ith speaker during the jth reference frame. $S_{i,k}$ estimates the value of the kth feature for the ith speaker. The average of the kth feature over all frames of all speakers is represented by U_k.

Features with larger F-ratios will be more useful for voice recognition. However, F-ratios are only valid for the set of data from which they were calculated. Features that appear to be useful for one set of speakers may be worthless for another set of speakers. To calculate meaningful F-ratios, a large population with a large number of examples from each speaker must be used.

Other methods for evaluating the usefulness of features exist. For example, the feature effectiveness criterion (FEC) is defined by Shridhar as follows [10]:

$$FEC = \sum \text{Interspeaker distances} - \sum \text{Intraspeaker distances}$$

Parameters with higher FEC values are more desirable since high interspeaker distances are favorable for discrimination and low intraspeaker distances are favorable for speaker variability. Another method for choosing which features to use in a voice-recognition system is simply to use recognition error rates of the system when different features are used as input. By using the same input speech data and pattern matching algorithm (algorithms will be discussed later in this chapter), the performance of different sets of parameters may be evaluated by comparison of recognition scores. Better parameters will yield better recognition scores. A broad range of testing must be used to prevent overtraining, which occurs when the system parameters are varied slightly in an attempt to achieve better performance on a specific set of input data, while the performance of the system actually drops for more general input data.

Distance Measures

Distance measures refer to methods of calculating differences between parameter vectors. Typically, one of the vectors is calculated from data of the unknown speaker while the other vector is calculated from that of a known speaker. However, some pattern-matching techniques require that vectors from the same speaker be compared to each other to determine the expected variance of the speaker in question. Descriptions of how distance measures are used will be presented later in this chapter.

Many different distance measures have been proposed, and deciding which one to use is as difficult as determining which set of parameters to use. Often, a method is chosen simply because it yields favorable results and/or compensates for the ineffectiveness of certain parameters within a feature vector.

Most distance measures are variations of either the Euclidean or Manhattan distance between two vectors.

Euclidean:

$$d(a,b) = \left(\sum_{i=1}^{p} (a_i - b_i)^2 \right)^{1/2}$$

Manhattan:

$$d(a,b) = \sum_{i=1}^{p} |a_i - b_i|$$

where a_i and b_i are ith components of the two vectors to be compared and p is the number of features to compare.

The Euclidean and Manhattan distance measures are not appropriate for comparing two vectors of LPC coefficients since the coefficients are not independent. However, the likelihood ratio distortion, which only applies to LPC coefficients, can be used. It is defined as follows:

$$d_{LR}(a,b) = \frac{\mathbf{b}^T \mathbf{R}_a \mathbf{b}}{\mathbf{a}^T \mathbf{R}_a \mathbf{a}} - 1$$

where $\mathbf{a}$ and $\mathbf{b}$ are vectors of LPC predictor coefficients, $\mathbf{R}_a$ is the Toeplitz autocorrelation matrix (a byproduct of the calculation of the predictor coefficients) associated with $\mathbf{a}$, and T is transpose [20]. The log likelihood distance can be computed as follows:

$$d_{LLR} = \log(d_{LR})$$

These two distance measures are effective ways of comparing vectors of LPC predictor coefficients.

Since cepstral coefficients are the most commonly used type of voice-recognition parameter, several distance measures for cepstral coefficients have been suggested. Most of these distance measures are simple variations of the weighted cepstral distance:

$$d(a,b) = \left(\sum_{i=1}^{p} [f_i(a_i - b_i)]^2 \right)^{1/2}$$

where, again, p is the number of features and f_i is the weighting function [21]. Several weighting functions have been suggested:

Uniform:

$$f_i = 1$$

Expected difference:

$$f_i = \frac{1}{E[a_i - b_i]}$$

where E is the expected difference between two features determined from a population of speakers.

Inverse variance:

$$f_i = \frac{1}{\text{var}(a_i)}$$

Uniform without first coefficient:

$$f_i = \begin{cases} 0 & \text{if } i = 1 \\ 1 & \text{if } 1 < i \le p \end{cases}$$

The expected difference and inverse variance weighting functions attempt to maximize the F-ratio of each feature. The uniform without first coefficient function discounts the first coefficient, which has been shown to contain little information for speaker recognition [21].

The number of different distance measures is as great as the number of different extracted parameter types. Some distance measures were designed for a specific type of parameter. Others were chosen to maximize the F-ratios of any given feature. However, most were chosen simply because of their favorable performance with specific pattern matching algorithms.

Pattern Recognition

Pattern recognition in voice-recognition systems consists of developing a database of information about known speakers (training) and determining if an unknown speaker is one of the known speakers (testing). The result of the pattern recognition step is a decision about an unknown speaker's identity. In the previous sections, we discussed feature extraction and distance measures. In this section, algorithms that use these features and distance measures for making voice-recognition decisions will be explained.

Testing Voice-Recognition Systems

To compare the relative performance of the different pattern-recognition techniques, a brief discussion on the testing of voice-recognition systems is necessary. Typically, the relative performance of voice-recognition systems is based on the error rates for either verification or identification tasks. Unfortunately, error rates can be misleading owing to the large number of variables involved in the testing process. Error rates are affected by the amount of training data (the length and number of training utterances), the amount of testing data, the number of known speakers, the quality of data (amount of noise in the speech signals), and other factors. Thus, comparing error rates reported in the literature of two voice-recognition systems may be misleading.

Many studies report the error rates of various systems with the same input conditions as baselines for comparisons. Then the error rates are more meaningful. In this section, we will report error rates only from studies in which baseline error rates are also available or in which the effects of changing a variable in the test conditions, such as test utterance length, are examined. To make comparisons of test results more meaningful, researchers have begun using standardized databases for testing voice-recognition systems. For example, the

TIMIT database[2], originally designed for testing speech recognition systems, can also be used for testing voice-recognition systems. It contains speech from 420 speakers—230 male and 190 female—from throughout the United States with the speakers segregated into eight dialect regions (DR1-DR8). For each speaker, there are recordings of 10 sentences, two of which (SA1 and SA2) are the same for all 420 speakers. The recordings are of excellent quality, with 16 bits of resolution, sampled at 16 kHz.

Several other databases specifically designed for voice recognition are gaining acceptance as standard test databases. Among these are the SPIDRE, YOHO, and KING databases [22]. Unfortunately, the currently available databases do not meet the needs of all researchers, so many nonstandard test databases are still used.

Pattern-Recognition Techniques

Pattern-recognition processes consist of training and testing. During training, a model of each known speaker must be created. Each model consists of a set of features extracted from utterances spoken by the individual. The exact form of the model will depend on the nature of the pattern-recognition algorithm used. During testing, a similar model is created for the unknown speaker. To make a decision, the pattern-recognition algorithm compares the model of the unknown speaker with models of known speakers. The basic structure of the voice-recognition pattern-recognition process is shown in Figure 2.3.

Many different types of speaker models and decision methods will be discussed in the sections that follow, such as long-term feature averages, vector quantization, hidden Markov models, neural networks, and segregating techniques.

---

2. Available from the Linguistic Data Consortium (LDC) at the University of Pennsylvania, 441 Williams Hall, Philadelphia, PA 19104-6305. Tel. (215) 898-0464. E-mail: ldc@unagi.cis.upenn.edu

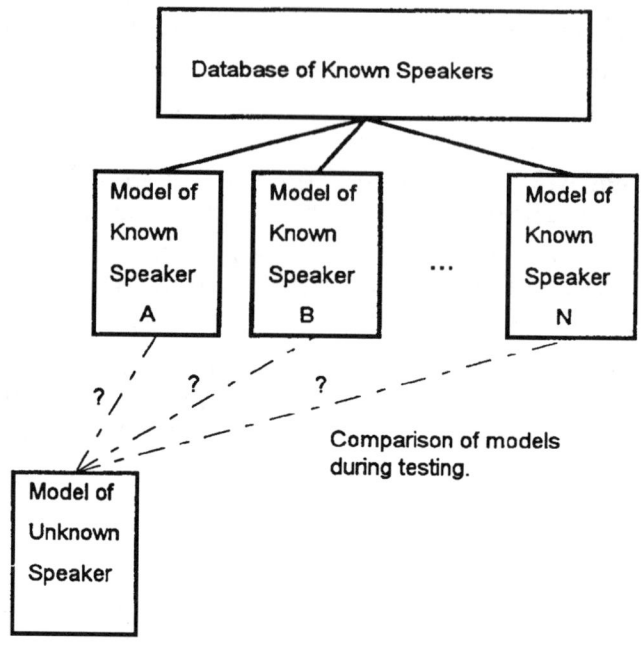

Figure 2.3 Voice-recognition pattern-recognition structure.

Long-term Averaging. One of the first modeling techniques proposed was long-term averaging of features. In this technique, a large number of feature vectors is obtained for each known speaker. The average and variance of each component of the feature vector are computed for all the examples from an individual. Thus, the model for each known speaker consists of two vectors: a vector of the average values of the example vectors and a vector of the variances. A similar model is made for an unknown speaker. The variance vectors are used for weighting each component of the average vectors in a manner related to the F-ratio of the features [23].

For closed-set identification, the decision is made by finding the model of a known speaker whose average vector is closest to the average vector of the unknown speaker. The distance between the two average vectors is computed using a weighted Euclidean distance measure. For verification, a decision criterion must be established. If the distance between the unknown and the known speaker is greater than the threshold value, the unknown is rejected. The criterion value must be adjusted so that the false acceptance error rate is as low as possible without increasing the false rejection error rate above an intolerable level.

The long-term averaging technique was designed for text-independent voice recognition. Its accuracy is highly dependent on the duration of the training and test utterances, which must be sufficiently long and varied. With shorter utterances, the intraspeaker variance increases owing to differences in the content of the utterances. For example, a short training utterance might contain a sentence in which mainly low vowels were used, such as "the cat sat on the mat." If the test utterance contained mainly high vowels instead, as in "he eats peas, beets, and kiwis," then the long-term average vectors for the two utterances would be different despite the fact that the vectors were generated from the same person's speech. Using the long-term averaging technique [24], an error rate of 80% was reported for 0.06 seconds of test data, 34% for 2.5 seconds of test data, and 6% for 40 seconds of test data. These experiments were all performed with 20 seconds of training data.

Researchers have used the long-term averaging approach with several different kinds of features, such as inverse filter spectral coefficients, pitch, and cepstral coefficients [25]. The inverse filter spectral coefficients were the most commonly used despite their susceptibility to channel variations [10,25].

The voice-recognition technique of using long-term averages of features yields favorable results when long utterance lengths are used and channel variance is small. Of course, its performance would be better if the training and testing text were the same, since the intraspeaker variance due to the content of the utterances would be reduced. Unfortunately, it is not always possible to control the training and testing utterances.

Vector Quantization. In the long-term averaging approach, each speaker's model consisted of a single cluster of data represented by an average and variance vector. However, this approach yields a high variance if the data actually contains multiple clusters. Since human speech is composed primarily of vowels, it is natural to expect clusters in a set of feature vectors. Each cluster is the result of the speaker generating the same sound each time a given vowel is pronounced.

Vector quantization (VQ) is an effective method of segregating data into clusters and determining the centroids of those clusters. VQ reduces a set of n k-dimensional vectors into a codebook of N centroid vectors where $n \gg N$. Linde, Buzo, and Gray developed an efficient algorithm for determining the codebook vectors [26]. The basic algorithm is specified as follows:

1. Initialize the N codebook vectors uniformly throughout the vector space by analyzing the sample data.
2. Partition the n training vectors into N groups by determining to which centroid each training vector is closest. Any distance measure may be used at this step.
3. Calculate the average distortion for each input vector using the same distance measure that was used in step (2). If the change since the last iteration of the average distortion is less then some threshold, e, then terminate.
4. Determine the new centroids of each of the partitions of input vectors and store these new values in the codebook. Go to (2).

VQ was originally designed for speech transmission systems to reduce the bandwidth of signals. Instead of transmitting all the bits necessary to represent the k-dimensional vector, only the codebook entry number of the centroid closest to the vector would need to be transmitted. Thus, a sequence of codebook entry numbers could be transmitted to represent an entire utterance. At the receiving end, an approximation of the original vector could be constructed by looking up the codebook entry of each number in the sequence. The codebook itself would only need to be transmitted once at the beginning of the message.

VQ can be used in many different ways in automatic speaker recognition. In some systems, VQ is used only to compress the data. In other systems, the segregation of vectors is used as a preprocessing step. However, the most common use of VQ is as a pattern-recognition method itself.

When VQ is used as a pattern-recognition method, a codebook is created for each known speaker by applying the VQ algorithm shown above to a set of feature vectors from the known speaker's training utterances. For text-independent identification, a comparison of the unknown's vectors is made with the codebooks of each known speaker. For each codebook, the minimum distortion of each vector in the test data to one of the vectors in the codebook is accumulated. The name of the codebook with the smallest accumulated distortion is returned as the identity of the unknown speaker. For text-independent verification, a similar procedure is followed. The accumulated distortion between the unknown and the codebook for the person to be verified is determined. If the distortion is above the criterion value, the unknown is rejected [20].

A similar approach may be used for text-dependent identification and verification. First, a codebook is created for each speaker using utterances of a prescribed text. Then, a sequence of codebook entries is determined for the same utterance—that is, encoded using the codebook. This sequence is called a *template*. During testing, the same prescribed text is spoken by the unknown person. For identification, the unknown is compared with all the stored sequences of codebook entry numbers. The accumulated distortion between the unknown and each stored sequences is calculated. The stored sequence with the lowest distortion is determined to be the same as the unknown [27]. For verification, a similar process is used with a criterion value for the distortion. During both identification and verification, a time-alignment process is used to remove variations in speaking rate of the prescribed text that might otherwise cause unwarranted distortion. Thus, using VQ for text-dependent voice recognition is very similar to the speech recognition of isolated words using dynamic time warping.

Using the VQ method described above introduces a new variable that affects performance—codebook size. With a codebook of only one vector, this technique is similar to long-term averaging of feature vectors. With larger codebooks, a speaker's voice can be better characterized, but at significant computational expense. F. K. Soong reports error rates of 20% for codebooks of size 4, 10% for size 8, and 2% for size 64 for identification based on utterances of 10 digits (thus only quasi-text-independent) in a noise-free environment [20].

VQ is a useful technique for automatic speaker recognition because of its ability to reduce the size of a data set dramatically with very little loss in accuracy.

Hidden Markov Models. Hidden Markov models (HMMs) are a useful method for modeling both the stationary and transient properties of a signal. They are appropriate for modeling speech because some speech sounds are sustained, such as vowels, while others are ephemeral, such as stop consonants, and the transitions between them are short periods of rapid change. Since HMMs are probabilistic by nature, they are able to represent accurately signals that exhibit such diverse behavior.

The basic structure of a HMM is a set of states with transitions between each state. For each transition from a given state, a probability of taking that transition is assigned. The sum of the probabilities of all transitions from a state must equal one. At each state, a symbol is outputted. The symbol to be outputted is also determined probabilistically. Thus, each state contains a probability distribution of the possible output symbols. These models are called "hidden" because the sequence of states is not directly observable. It can only be probabilistically deduced from the sequence of output symbols, which is all that can be observed. HMMs display the *Markov* property since the probability of taking any transition is not based on any previous behavior but only on the current state of the system.

Formally, an HMM may be defined as follows [28]:

N = The number of states in the model;

M = The number of output symbols in the model;

$Q = \{q_1, q_2, \ldots, q_N\}$, the states in the model;

$A = \{a_{ij}\}$, $a_{ij} = \Pr(q_j$ at $t + 1 | q_i$ at $t)$,
the state transition probability distribution;

$B = \{b_j(k)\}$, $b_j(k) = \Pr(v_k$ at $t | q_j$ at $t)$, the output symbol probability distribution at state j, where $\{v_k\}$ is the set of output symbols;

$\pi = \{\pi_i\}$, $\pi_i = \Pr(q_i$ at $t = 0)$, the initial state distribution.

The formal model for the HMM shown in Figure 2.4 would be:

$N = 2$

$M = 2$

$Q = \{q_1 =$ "State 1", $q_2 =$ "State 2"$\}$

$A = \{a_{11} = 0.5, a_{12} = 0.5, a_{21} = 0.7, a_{22} = 0.3\}$

$B = \{b_1(O_1)=0.1, b_1(O_2)=0.9, b_2(O_1)=0.3, b_2(O_2)0.7\}$

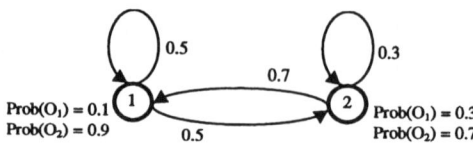

Figure 2.4 Two-state ergotic HMM.

The π distribution was not shown in Figure 2.4; however, if we assume that starting in state 1 or state 2 is equally likely, then:

$$\pi = \{\pi_1 = 0.5,\ \pi_2 = 0.5\}$$

Using this model, an output sequence, $O = \{o_0, o_1, \ldots o_{t-1}\}$, can be created by first choosing an initial state according to the initial state distribution π. Then, for each time step, a symbol is outputted according to the distribution B and a transition is taken according to distribution A for the current state. A random number generator is necessary for determining the outcome of each choice. If a generator that returns evenly distributed numbers in the range $0.0 \leq x < 1.0$ is used, then a value returned from the random number generator <0.5 would indicate starting in state 1, while a value ≥ 0.5 would indicate starting in state 2. Transition and output choice may be determined in a similar fashion.

Many topologies of HMMs are possible. HMMs that contain transitions to and from every state with nonzero probability are called *ergotic* models, since they often exhibit so-called ergotic behavior; that is, the probability that each state will be revisited approaches 1 as time increases, and revisits do not necessarily occur at periodically spaced intervals [28].

Other topologies may be formed by forcing certain transitions of an ergotic model to have probabilities of zero. For example, the HMM in Figure 2.5 would have:

$$a_{13} = 0,\ a_{21} = 0,\ a_{31} = 0,\ a_{32} = 0$$

Notice that state 3 of the left-to-right HMM in Figure 2.5 is an *absorbing state* that cannot be exited once entered. The use of left-to-right, circular (Figure 2.6), and other topologies have been described in the literature [29,30].

There are three basic problems related to HMMs:

1. *The recognition problem:* Given an output sequence and a model, what is the probability that the model could have created the sequence?
2. *The sequence problem:* Given an output sequence and a model, what is the most likely sequence of states that could have created the output sequence?
3. *The training problem:* Given an output sequence and a topology, how can the parameters of a model—that is, the probability distributions for transitions and outputs—be adjusted to maximize the probability that the model created the output sequence?

An algorithm that solves the *recognition problem* can be used for recognition tasks by comparing new data to the models of known signals. A solution to the *sequence problem* can

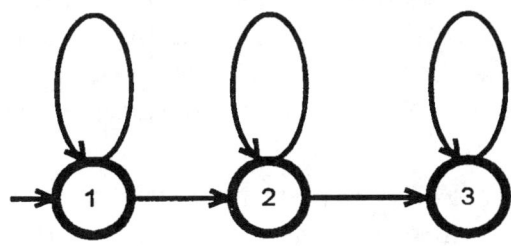

Figure 2.5 Left-to-right HMM.

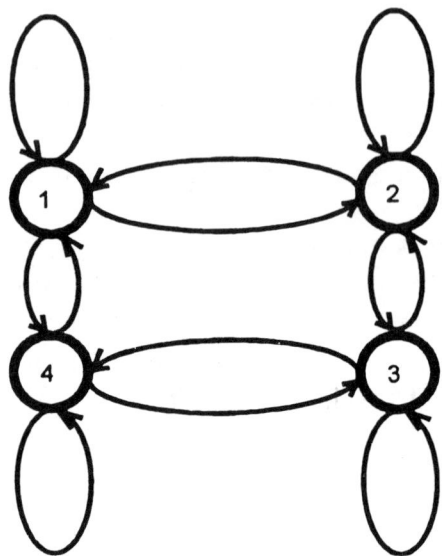

Figure 2.6 Circular HMM.

be used for applications in which each state has a specific meaning. For example, each state might be related to a broad phonetic category, such as vowels or plosives. Finally, the solution to the *training problem* will allow us to train a HMM for a given input sequence. Efficient recursive and iterative algorithms have been developed for solving these three problems [28].

The models described thus far have assumed that discrete output symbols were used. These are called *discrete HMMs*. However, the output sequence need not consist of a set of discrete symbols. *Continuous HMMs* use a probability distribution for each component of the parameter vectors at each state.

Text-Dependent Voice Recognition. When HMMs are used for text-dependent voice recognition, the process is similar to the way in which HMMs are used for small-vocabulary, isolated-word recognition. One HMM is trained for each individual uttering the prescribed text, using the solution to the training problem. When an unknown sample of speech is to be recognized, the solution to the recognition problem is used for determining which model of a known speaker has the highest probability of generating the unknown sample.

HMMs used for text-dependent recognition may be either discrete or continuous. If the models are discrete, then a vector quantizer is used to convert each feature vector into the index number of the vector in the codebook that most closely matches the feature vector. Thus, the number of output symbols for the model, M, is equal to the size of the codebook. If the model is continuous, then the distributions of the actual feature vector values are used for B and the output at each state will be a feature vector.

Text-dependent voice-recognition systems (and small-vocabulary, isolated-word recognition systems) typically use left-to-right HMMs. The ordering of states models the order of speech events during the prescribed text. Since the prescribed text is spoken during both training and testing, the ordering of speech events should be the same. Left-to-right HMMs are also able to model the duration of speech events by using the transitions from each state back to itself. (See Figure 2.5.)

Many experimental studies have tested the performance of text-dependent HMM-based voice-recognition systems. In 1989, an error rate of 4.6% was reported for an HMM-based system using data recorded over long-distance telephone lines [31]. As a baseline, the paper reported an error rate of 6.2% for a template-based system using the same input. Other experiments resulted in an error rate of 3.5% for an HMM-based system using 1.1-second test utterances with 66 seconds of training data versus 6.7% for a template-based approach using the same input data [11].

Text-Independent Voice Recognition. HMMs have also been used for text-independent voice recognition. In these systems, either ergotic or circular models are used. The states are trained to represent different phonetic classes, such as strong vocalization, silence, or nasal [11]. Since more transitions are possible in these models than in left-to-right models, no ordering of speech events is imposed. Therefore, during training and testing, the individuals may speak any text.

During training, the parameters of a model are adjusted to represent best the salient features of each person's speech. If enough training data is used, the model parameters will stabilize. An HMM is trained for each known speaker. During testing, the solution to the recognition problem is used to determine which model is most likely to generate the unknown input.

Experimental results show that text-independent voice-recognition systems using HMMs can be expected to perform slightly better than systems using VQ. One experimenter reported identification error rates of 4.4% for a system based on continuous HMMs versus 4.6% for a VQ system [32]. In the same experiment, a system based on discrete HMMs produced an identification error rate of 11.7%. These experiments were performed with 40 seconds of training data and 20 seconds of test data with 36 speakers. Another experimenter reported similar results for verification tasks [33]. In all, experimental results show that HMM-based systems perform slightly better than text-independent systems based on VQ.

In the applications of HMMs described so far, one HMM was used to represent the speech of each individual. These types of models may be called *utterance unit models*, since each model represents the entire utterance given by the individual. Rosenberg proposed using *subword unit models* for voice recognition. The subword could either be phone-like units (PLUs), in which a phonetic transcription of the training data is required, or acoustic segment units (ASUs), in which segmentation of speech segments is performed automatically [34]. Recognition of a speaker would be performed by recognizing a series of subword units. This method would be similar to large-vocabulary, continuous-speech recognition, in which models of words are the concatenation of subword units. A voice-recognition system based on subword unit models could be either text-dependent or text-independent.

Preprocessing. HMMs have also been used as a preprocessor for voice-recognition systems that segregate feature vectors by phonetic category. The details of segregating systems will be discussed later.

Summary of HMMs. HMMs have been successfully used in voice recognition. Utterance unit models have been used for both text-dependent and text-independent recognition systems. Other research has been carried out to examine the use of subword unit models for recognition. HMMs are also used in the preprocessing stages of voice-recognition systems that segregate feature vectors by phonetic category.

Neural Networks. Artificial neural networks (NNs) are computational models that attempt to emulate the human brain by a topology that resembles interconnected nerve cells. NNs are capable of modeling nonlinearity and can be used for many different tasks, such as classification, associative memory, and clustering. This versatility has allowed them to solve problems in areas as diverse as computer vision, process control, and medical diagnosis [35]. The main drawback of neural networks is their long training time. Although knowledge about neural networks is still in an early stage, their application to automatic speaker recognition is significant.

An NN consists of a collection of neurons (also called perceptrons or nodes) that are connected by weighted pathways. Each neuron is a processing element that has many inputs, performs one function, and produces one output. The computation performed by a typical neuron consists of taking the sum of its inputs and using that value as the argument to a nonlinear function. (See Figure 2.7.)

This nonlinear function is called the *activation function* of the neuron. The most commonly used activation function is the *sigmoid*:

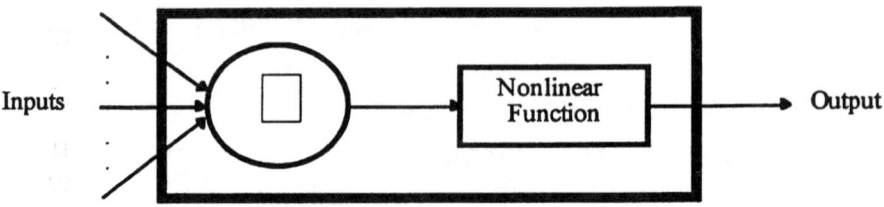

Figure 2.7 A typical neuron.

$$f(x) = \frac{1}{1 + e^{-\lambda x}} \tag{2.5}$$

where λ is > 0. The constant λ determines how "hard" the activation function limits the input. The "hardness" of the activation may be viewed graphically as the slope of the transition in Figure 2.8. Steeper slopes indicate a harder activation function, which results in faster changes in the output value in response to changes in the input value.

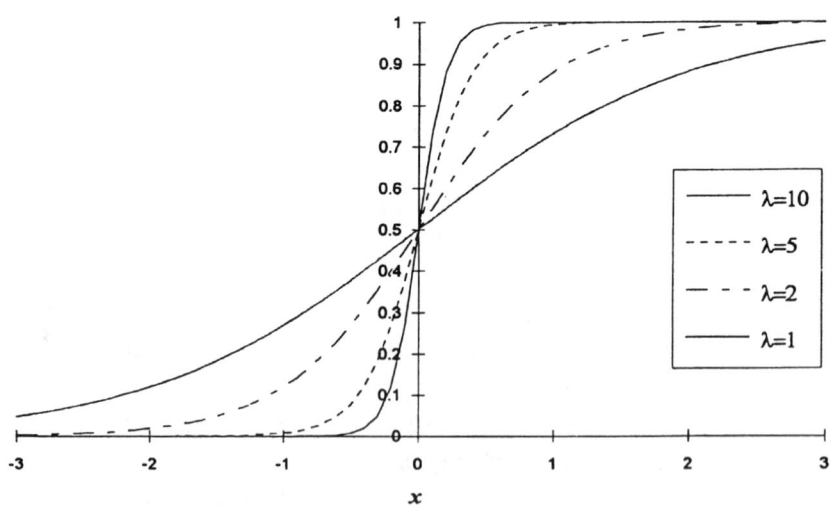

Figure 2.8 The sigmoidal activation function.

The most commonly used neural networks, called *multilayer feedforward networks*, consist of multiple layers of neurons connected by weighted pathways. The networks as a whole have multiple inputs and one or more outputs. The pathways connect neurons from one layer of the network to the next layer closer to the output layer.

The network shown in Figure 2.9 has three input neurons $\{z_1, z_2, z_3\}$ and two output neurons, $\{o_1, o_2\}$. This network is fully connected—that is, the output of each neuron is used as an input for every neuron in the next layer of the network. This network contains one hidden layer of three neurons $\{y_1, y_2, y_3\}$. Since each neuron has only one output value, this value may be given the same name as the neuron. Thus, the output value of neuron z_1 is also called z_1. The weights are shown as $v_{i,j}$ for the first layer and $w_{j,k}$ for the second layer.

The scheme suggested in Figure 2.7 may be used for determining how to calculate the output values for each neuron. The input neurons do not perform any calculation but simply pass through the input values to the next layer. The output of y_1 can be calculated as follows:

$$y_1 = f\left(\sum_{j=1}^{3} v_{1,j} z_j\right)$$

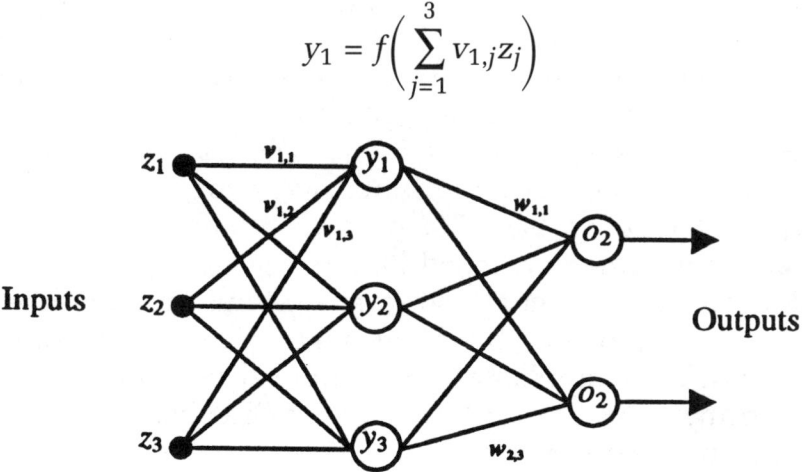

Figure 2.9 A multilayer feedforward neural network.

where $f(\ )$ is the activation function for the neuron, $v_{1,j}$ is the weight of the connection from neuron j, and z_j is the output of neuron j. The outputs of the other neurons can be calculated in a similar fashion. The process of calculating the output values of the network by evaluating the outputs at each layer is called *feedforward recall*.

Training NNs. Like HMMs, NNs must be trained before they are useful. The common way to train a multilayer network is to use error back-propagation training. Before a network is trained, its weights are initialized to small random values. A set of input values and expected output values for those inputs is presented to the network. An iterative gradient descent approach is used for adjusting weights to minimize the differences between the desired output values and the output values calculated by the network using current weights and input.

For each training example, the error at the output layer is fed back to the previous layer and then fed back, layer by layer, until the input layer is reached. Each time an error value is fed back, the weights at that connection are adjusted slightly to reduce the error. A constant, α, determines how large a change in weights can be made during each iteration. This constant is called the *learning rate*.

As the process is repeated many times for the entire network and for the entire set of training examples, the output errors tend to decrease. The process is complete when a desired error value is reached [35].

Many factors affect the performance and training time of NNs, including the number of layers, the number of neurons in each layer, the number of connections between layers, and the learning rate. Currently, no theoretical basis exists for determining the optimal values for these variables. Thus, they are determined by trial-and-error or by heuristics.

Another concern about NNs is the possibility of overtraining. Overtraining occurs when too many training iterations are performed on a network, causing the network to learn coincidental patterns in the input. Overtraining causes a network to generalize poorly.

Voice Recognition With NNs. One of the first experimental voice-recognition systems using neural networks was proposed by Oglesby [36]. In this system, a feedforward network was created for each known speaker. Each network contained one output that was trained to be active (output approximately equal to 1) for input belonging to the speaker whom the network was supposed to represent. The output was trained to be inactive (output approximately equal to 0) for input belonging to other speakers. Thus, the training data included positive examples from the speaker in question as well as negative examples from other speakers in the population. The input to this network was a vector of 10 LPC-derived cepstral coefficients.

For speaker identification testing, each input vector was fed forward through the networks of all the known speakers. The output values for each network were accumulated. The network with the highest accumulated score was deemed to be the best match. For speaker verification, the input vectors for the unknown were fed forward through the network belonging to the individual wishing to be verified. If the average output value were greater than a threshold value, the unknown speaker was accepted.

Oglesby performed many tests to determine optimal parameters of NNs. He determined that single-hidden-layer networks outperformed double-hidden-layer networks (error rates of 8% versus 10%). Oglesby also determined that a large number of hidden nodes increased performance. The best error rate was obtained with 16 input nodes and 128 hidden nodes. Oglesby claimed that for small model sizes, his neural network approach outperformed VQ systems [36].

Rudasi and Zahorian presented two other possible strategies for using NNs to perform voice recognition [37]. Their first strategy was to use one large network with one output per known speaker. During training, examples from each speaker were presented to the network. When a particular speaker's input vectors were presented to the network, the expected value for the output corresponding to that speaker was set to one. All other outputs were set to zero.

During identification testing, the average output scores for all of the unknown input vectors were determined. The best match was the speaker with the highest average output value. Verification can be performed by comparing average output values to a criterion value.

The "one large network" strategy has several problems. Although it will perform well for small populations of speakers, performance and training times for large populations would be less than satisfactory. When new speakers are added to the population, the entire network must be retrained. Rudasi and Zahorian's second strategy was to use small *binary networks*, each of which was required to make a distinction between only two speakers, thus taking modularity to an extreme. Although there were now many more networks, the training time for each network was very short. If the population included N speakers, then $N * (N - 1)/2$ binary networks were required. Since each network was responsible for only a small portion of the overall classification, the binary networks could be highly specialized and offer much better performance than a large network.

Binary classifiers may be used in two different ways. The simplest method is to process the unknown data with all the binary networks. The output of each network can be considered to be a vote. The vote need not be a hard decision but can be a score reflecting confidence in the decision. The known speaker with the most votes is determined to be the best match. This approach is called *global soft-decision search*.

A second approach is to perform a *binary tree search*. This approach requires a series of elimination rounds similar to tournaments in sporting events. The winners of each round proceed to the next round of competition until only one winner is left. The binary tree search requires less computation than the global soft-decision search. However, the two methods will produce the same answer if all the binary networks are 100% accurate. Although binary classifiers are valuable for closed-set identification problems with large populations, they cannot be used for verification tasks.

Time-Delayed NNs. In the NN models described so far, the input was given in terms of short-time input vectors—that is, one frame of features at a time. This approach neglects the transient information that may be useful for voice recognition. Earlier in the chapter, we mentioned how HMMs captured transient information that could not be represented with VQ models. Similarly, time-delayed NNs (TDNNs) were developed to capture transient information with an NN approach.

The input for TDNNs is actually a series of feature vectors called a *frame*. Bennani describes a system in which the input consists of a 25-window-wide analysis frame in which each input window overlaps the previous window by 24 of the 25 points [38].

The TDNN system described by Bennani was not a fully connected network. The input neurons were positioned as an array (25 time units × 16 features). Each row of neurons in the hidden layer was connected to only five consecutive rows (in the time-step dimension) of input neurons. Bennani's system had a 21 × 12 neuron hidden layer. Bennani's identification error rate was 2% for 20 speakers using five TIMIT database sentences for training and five for testing.

Summary of NNs. As more knowledge is gained about NNs, their applicability to voice recognition is sure to increase. Several approaches have been tested: large discriminating networks, binary networks, and TDNNs. Because of the promising results, research in this area is expected to continue.

Segregating Systems. Segregating voice-recognition systems treat the text-independent speaker-recognition task as a two-step process. First, all input vectors are segregated into groups based on certain spectral characteristics, generally ones associated with particular classes of speech sounds. Then, for each group of vectors, the vectors from each known individual are compared with vectors from the unknown. The basic idea is to compare a specific sound class produced by the unknown speaker with the same sound class produced by the known speakers. Since segregating systems require two steps, two questions must be answered during their design: "How are vectors segregated?" and "How are vectors within each group compared?" Through the answer to the first question, the answer to the second becomes apparent. Variations on techniques discussed previously, such as VQ and HMMs, are used for solving these problems.

In the first study proposing a segregating approach, vowel samples were segregated manually [39]. Vowel classification was performed by human operators assisted by computer programs that identified likely locations for vowels. LPC coefficients were calculated at the steady state position of each vowel. Then, the vectors were compared using a weighted Euclidean distance measure.

Fakotakis discussed a system in which vowels are located by looking for peaks in the short-time energy contours of utterances [40]. Cepstral coefficients are calculated at each vowel locus and used as input to a vector quantizer that segregates the feature vectors. Each vector is placed in the group corresponding to the nearest centroid in the codebook. Wang describes a similar segregating voice-recognition system that uses VQ for an entire utterance, not just the vowels [41].

If VQ is used for segregation and the distance from the centroid is used for comparison, then the method behaves like the VQ recognition process described earlier. Thus, most VQ segregating systems use distance measures weighted by the variance within each group of vectors [41].

Another method for segregating vectors uses HMMs. Savic describes a method in which ergotic HMMs are used for representing broad phonetic categories such as vowels or fricatives [42]. Each state in the HMM is associated with a category. To segregate the vectors of an utterance, the solution to the HMM sequence problem (for example, "What is the most likely sequence of states for a sequence of observations?") is used. Thus, each vector is assigned to one of the states in the HMM. To compare vectors within each group, a Bayesian classifier is used. Therefore, the mean vector and covariance matrix is required. The final score is a weighted summation of the scores from each group.

Matsui suggests a system in which vectors are segregated using either a voiced/un-voiced classifier or an ergotic HMM for determining broad phonetic categories. Within each group, VQ is used for performing recognition. Thus, each known speaker has several codebooks, one for each category [43].

Kao discusses a similar system [44]. However, in his implementation, a speaker-independent continuous-speech recognizer is used for segregating vectors. The output of the recognizer is a hypothesized phonetic category. VQ codebooks for each speaker are created for each possible category.

Many segregating voice-recognition systems have been developed. These systems use a combination of techniques, such as VQ and HMMs. However, as of this writing, segregating systems that use neural networks have not been discussed in the literature. This would appear to be a promising area of research.

Miscellaneous Pattern-Matching Techniques. In preceding sections, many voice-recognition pattern-matching techniques have been discussed. These techniques include long-term feature averaging, VQ, HMMs, NNs, and segregating systems.

Many other miscellaneous pattern-matching techniques have been discussed in the literature. For example, principal component analysis is a technique for optimizing dynamic time warping systems [45]. Similarly, orthogonalization has been used for improving the performance of long-term averaging recognizers [12]. Several statistical detection approaches have been examined, such as probability density functions [46,47], trajectory space comparisons [48], k-nearest neighbors [15,49], discriminator counting [15,49], Gaussian mixture models [50], Fourier Bessel functions [51], and probabilistic acoustic maps [52,53].

Unfortunately, comparing the performance of voice-recognition systems is difficult owing to variations in testing. Error rates are affected by many features, such as noise, training time, testing time, number of speakers, and definition of free text.

A common feature of all voice-recognition pattern-matching techniques discussed in this section is that they perform a considerable amount of data reduction, essentially some kind of averaging. Data reduction is necessary to extract the salient features of an individual's speech and also to make the recognition process computationally feasible.

VOICE RECOGNITION IN NOISY ENVIRONMENTS

Overcoming the difficulties associated with performing voice recognition in noisy environments is a primary concern. For voice recognition to be successful when performed over telephone lines—perhaps the most important general application area—voice-recognition systems need to be relatively impervious to noise. Several studies in this area have been completed [54–56]. Experiments over radio channels have also been performed [47,57].

The main difficulty with noisy environments is not the noise itself, but the variations in the noise. An extreme example occurs when a voice-recognition system is trained on clean speech—that is, speech containing no noise—and is tested on noisy speech. Error rates are bound to be higher when any aspect of the signal processing is changed between training and testing. These include the type of microphone, the amount of ambient noise, and the transmission medium.

If the same noise appears in both training and testing, however, it will not be a factor unless the signal-to-noise ratio (SNR) is low.

Typical channel variations are changes in the amount of additive noise, bandpass filtering, and phase distortion applied to the actual speech signal. To make voice-recognition systems immune to such variations, several techniques have been devised, including selection of features with immunity to channel variations and preprocessing of signals to separate the noise components of a signal from the actual speech component.

In an earlier section of this chapter, the feature selection process was described, and several types of features used for voice recognition were listed. In addition to the techniques for feature selection already described, some features have been used or invented for use based solely on their immunity to channel variation.

For example, fundamental frequency (pitch) and formant frequencies have been used because they are not affected by additive noise or phase distortion and are affected only slightly by the bandpass filtering typical of communication channels [58,59]. Cepstral coefficients are used because they are unaffected by linear distortion.

Delta-type features have also been used. These are calculated by determining the difference between successive vectors and using the difference vectors as features. Delta-type features automatically remove the bias from a signal.

Other features mentioned in the literature specifically for their immunity to channel variance are clipped autocorrelation coefficients [54] and relative spectral perceptual linear predictive (RASTA-PLP) methods [13,14].

To separate an additive noise component of a signal from the components useful for voice recognition, the communication channel must first be characterized. The simplest method for characterizing a channel in text-dependent applications is to determine the average value of all features over the entire utterance. Then, the average vectors can be subtracted from each vector in the utterance to normalize it [60]. This technique is also useful for compensating for some of the bandpass filtering. However, if the utterances are short, some of the speaker-dependent information will also be removed from the signal.

Another method is to characterize the additive noise from segments of the utterance where no speech is present, ensuring that actual speech will not be mistakenly classified as stationary channel noise. Alternately, Wang suggests averaging channel characteristics over many different types of channels instead of over time [41].

Filtering signals during preprocessing can be useful for removing variance in the bandpass filtering behavior of the communication channel. Successful results have been achieved by attenuating certain spectral regions during preprocessing that are likely to be attenuated by some, but not all, communication channels, thus achieving normalization [44,61]. The same effect results from attenuating cepstral coefficients, a process called *liftering* [13].

Gish suggests that the channel should be modeled statistically as a Gaussian random vector, which can then be incorporated into the classifier, assuming that a Gaussian probability distribution function classifier (GPDF) is used [55]. By choosing features that are immune to channel effects or by removing channel effects before features are extracted, voice-recognition systems can be designed to perform better in noisy environments.

SUMMARY

In this chapter, previous research in voice recognition was presented. The early use of voiceprints was discussed. The different types of features, distance measures, and pattern-matching techniques were explained. Finally, studies on performing voice recognition in noisy environments were summarized.

References

[1] Kersta, L. G., "Voiceprint Identification," *Nature*, Vol. 196 No. 4861, 29 December 1962, pp. 1253–1257.
[2] Bolt, Richard H. et al., "Identification of a Speaker by Speech Spectrograms," *Science*, Vol. 166, Oct. 1969.
[3] Koenig, Bruce E., "Spectrographic Voice Identification: A Forensic Survey," JASA, Vol. 79 No. 6, June 1986, pp. 2088–2090.
[4] Tetschner, W. *Voice Processing*, 2nd ed., Norwood, MA: Artech House, 1993.
[5] Rabiner, Lawrence R., and Schafer, Ronald W., *Digital Processing of Speech Signal*, Englewood Cliffs, NJ: Prentice-Hall, Inc., 1978.
[6] Pruzansky, S., and Mathews, M. V., "Talker-Recognition Procedure Based on Analysis of Variance," *JASA* 36, 1964, pp. 2041–2047.
[7] Atal, B. S., "Speech Analysis and Synthesis by Linear Prediction of Speech Wave," *JASA* 47, 65(A), 1970.
[8] Atal, B. S., "Effectiveness of Linear Prediction Characteristics of the Speech Wave for Automatic Speaker Identification and Verification," *JASA*, Vol. 55, June 1974, pp. 1304–1312.
[9] Fasolo, L. and Mian, G. A., "A Comparison Between Two Approaches to Automatic Speaker Recognition," *ICASSP*, 1978, pp. 275–278.
[10] Shridhar, M. et al., "Text-Independent Speaker Recognition Using Orthogonal Linear Prediction," *ICASSP*, 1981, pp. 197–200.
[11] Rosenberg, Aaron E. et al., "Connected Word Talker Verification Using Whole Word Hidden Markov Models," *ICASSP*, 1991, pp. 381–384.
[12] Mohankrishnan, N. et al. "A Composite Scheme for Text-Independent Speaker Recognition," *ICASSP*, 1982, pp. 1653–1656.
[13] Kao, Yu-Hung et al., "Robustness Study of Free-Text Speaker Identification and Verification," *ICASSP*, 1993, pp. 379–382.
[14] Openshaw, J.P. et al., "A Comparison of Composite Features Under Degraded Speech in Speaker Recognition," *ICASSP*, 1993, pp. 371–374.
[15] Nakasone, H. and Melvin, C., "Computer Assisted Voice Identification System," *ICASSP*, 1988, pp. 587–590.
[16] Xu, L. et al., "The Optimization of Perceptually Based Features for Speaker Identification," *ICASSP*, 1989, pp. 520–523.
[17] Liu, Chi-Shi et al., "Study of Line Spectrum Pair Frequencies for Speaker Recognition," *ICASSP*, 1990, pp. 277–280.

[18] Attili, Joseph B. et al., "A TMS32020-Based Real-Time, Text-Independent Automatic Speaker Verification System," *ICASSP*, 1988, pp. 599–602.
[19] Wilber, JoEllen and Taylor, Fred J., "Consistent Speaker Identification via Wigner Smoothing Techniques," *ICASSP*, 1988, pp. 591–593.
[20] Soong, F. K. et al., "A Vector Quantization Approach to Speaker Recognition," *ICASSP*, 1985, pp. 387–390.
[21] Velius, George, "Variant of Cepstrum-Based Speaker Identity Verification," *ICASSP*, 1988, pp. 583–586.
[22] Godfrey, J. et al., "Public Databases for Speaker Recognition and Verification," *ESCA Workshop on Automatic Speaker Recognition, Identification, and Verification*, 1994.
[23] Markel, John D. and Davis, Steven B., "Text-Independent Speaker Identification from a Large Linguistically Unconstrained Time-Spaced Data Base," *ICASSP*, 1978, pp. 287–289.
[24] Wrench, E. H., "A Realtime Implementation of a Text-Independent Speaker Recognition System," *ICASSP*, 1981, pp. 193–196.
[25] Doddington, George R., "Speaker Recognition—Identifying People by Their Voices," *Proceedings of the IEEE*, Vol. 73 No. 11, Nov. 1985, pp. 1651–1663.
[26] Linde, Y., Buzo, A., and Gray, R., "An Algorithm for Vector Quantizer Design," *IEEE Transactions on Communications*, Vol. COM-28 No. 1, Jan. 1980, pp. 84–95.
[27] Buck, Joseph et al., "Text-Dependent Speaker Recognition Using Vector Quantization," *ICASSP*, 1985, pp. 391–394.
[28] Rabiner, Lawrence R. and Juang, B.H., "An Introduction to Hidden Markov Models," *IEEE Transactions on Acoustics, Speech, and Signal Processing*, Jan. 1986, pp. 4–16.
[29] Zheng, Yuan-Cheng and Yuan, Bao-Zong, "Text-Dependent Speaker Identification Using Circular Hidden Markov Models," *ICASSP*, 1988, pp. 580–582.
[30] Lee, K.-F., *Automatic Speech Recognition*, Boston, MA: Kluwer Academic Publishers. 1989.
[31] Naik, Jayant M. et al., "Speaker Verification over Long Distance Telephone Lines," *ICASSP*, 1989, pp. 524–527.
[32] Matsui, Tomoko and Furui, Sadaoki, "Comparison of Text-Independent Speaker Recognition Methods Using VQ Distortion and Discrete/Continuous HMMs," *ICASSP*, 1992, pp. 157–160.
[33] Tishby, N., "On the Application of Mixture AR Hidden Markov Models to Text Independent Speaker Recognition," *IEEE Trans. Signal Processing*, SP-39, 1991, 563–570.

[34] Rosenberg, Aaron E. et al., "Sub-Word Unit Talk Verification Using Hidden Markov Models," *ICASSP*, 1990, pp. 269–272.
[35] Zurada, Jacek W., *Introduction to Artificial Neural Systems*, St. Paul, MN: West Publishing Co., 1992.
[36] Oglesby, J. and Mason, J. S., "Optimization of Neural Models for Speaker Identification," *ICASSP*, 1990.
[37] Rudasi, Laszlo and Zahorian, Stephen A., "Text-Independent Talker Identification with Neural Networks," *ICASSP*, 1991, pp. 389–392.
[38] Bennani, Younes and Gallinari, Patrick, "On the Use of TDNN-Extracted Features Information in Talker Identification," *ICASSP*, 1991, pp. 385–388.
[39] Pfeifer, Larry L., "New Techniques for Text-Independent Speaker Identification," *ICASSP*, 1978, pp. 283–286.
[40] Fakotakis, N., Tsopanoglou, A., and Kokkinakis, G., "A Text-Independent Speaker Recognition System Based on Vowel Spotting," *Speech Communication*, Vol 12, 1993, pp. 57–68.
[41] Wang, H. et al., "A Novel Approach to Speaker Identification over Telephone Networks," *ICASSP*, 1993, pp. 407–410.
[42] Savic, Michael and Gupta, Sunil K., "Variable Parameter Speaker Verification System Based on Hidden Markov Modeling," *ICASSP*, 1990, pp. 281–284.
[43] Matsui, Tomoko and Furui, Sadaoki, "A Text-Independent Speaker Recognition Method Robust against Utterance Variations," *ICASSP*, 1991, pp. 377–380.
[44] Kao, Yu-Hung et al., "Free-Text Speaker Identification over Long-Distance Telephone Channels Using Hypothesized Phonetic Segmentation," *ICASSP*, 1992, pp. 177–180.
[45] Naik, Jayant M. and Doddington, George R. "High Performance Speaker Verification Using Principal Spectral Components," *ICASSP*, 1986, pp. 881–884.
[46] Schwartz, R. et al. "The Application of Probability Density Estimation to Text-Independent Speaker Identification," *ICASSP*, 1982, pp. 1649–1652.
[47] Wolf, J. et al. "Further Investigation of Probabilistic Methods for Text-Independent Speaker Identification," *ICASSP*, 1983, pp. 551–554.
[48] Gong, Yifan and Haton, Jean-Paul, "Text-Independent Speaker Recognition by Trajectory Space Comparison," *ICASSP*, 1990, pp. 285–288.
[49] Higgins, A. L. et al., "Voice Identification Using Nearest-Neighbor Distance Measure," *ICASSP*, 1993, Vol. 2, pp. 375–378.

[50] Reynolds, D. A. and Rose, R. C., "An Integrated Speech-Background Model for Robust Speaker Identification," *ICASSP*, 1992, pp. 185–188.
[51] Gaganelis, D. A. and Frangoulis, E. D., "A Novel Approach to Speaker Verification," *ICASSP*, 1991, pp. 373–376.
[52] Tseng, Belle L. et al., "Continuous Probabilistic Acoustic Map for Speaker Recognition," *ICASSP*, 1992, pp. 161–164.
[53] Chang, Harry M., "Augmented Phonetic Map for Voice Verification," *ICASSP*, 1992, pp. 169–172.
[54] Ney, H., "Telephone-Line Speaker Recognition Using Clipped Autocorrelation Analysis," *ICASSP*, 1981, pp. 188–192.
[55] Gish, H. et al., "Investigation of Text-Independent Speaker Identification over Telephone Channels," *ICASSP*, 1985, pp. 379–382.
[56] Gish, H. et al., "Methods and Experiments for Text-Independent Speaker Recognition over Telephone Channels," *ICASSP*, 1986, pp. 865–868.
[57] Krasner, M. et al., "Investigation of Text-Independent Speaker Identification Techniques under Conditions of Variable Data," *ICASSP*, 1984.
[58] Hunt, Melvyn J., "Further Experiments in Text-Independent Speaker Recognition over Communication Channels," *ICASSP*, 1983, pp. 563–566.
[59] Federico, A. et al., "A New Automated Method for Reliable Speaker Identification and Verification over Telephone Channels," *ICASSP*, 1987, pp. 1457–1460.
[60] Rosenberg, A. E. and Soong, F. K., "Recent Research in Automatic Speaker Recognition," *Advances in Speech Signal Processing*, New York: Marcel Dekker, Inc., 1992.
[61] Rose, R. C. et al., "Robust Speaker Identification in Noisy Environments Using Noise Adaptive Speaker Models," *ICASSP*, 1991, pp. 401–404.

Methods of Context-Free Voice Recognition   3

In this chapter we present a description of the methods used for implementing a context-free (also called *text-independent*) voice-recognition system. To have a test-bed for our methods, we targeted applications in the area of law enforcement. We will state the goals of such a system along with the constraints imposed on it by the forensic applications.

The law-enforcement arena is arguably the most difficult area for voice recognition. Not only is the data difficult to collect—from such sources as hidden microphones, wiretaps, or telephone recording devices—but it also tends to be of poor quality. Moreover, the demands for accuracy imposed by the justice system often exceed those required for industrial applications.

Within the forensic context, then, we discuss and illustrate an ideal voice-recognition system. We delineate the various factors that prevent these ideal systems from being built at present, but we also suggest methods for overcoming some of the limitations.

We then detail the implementation of one of the voice-recognition systems we have actually built. The chapter concludes with a discussion of the logistics of forensic voice recognition.

VOICE RECOGNITION IN LAW ENFORCEMENT

When we began our research into context-free voice recognition, we needed a particular application on which to focus, and we chose the area of law enforcement for several reasons. First, the challenges there were greatest. The speakers to be recognized are either unaware of their participation and so make no effort to speak clearly or, if they are aware, tend to be uncooperative. The voice data may be scanty—a 12-second recorded bomb threat, for example—and what there is of it is usually of poor quality. The data limitations forced us to carry the notion of text independence to its extreme; we needed to build a system in which absolutely any speech could be used both for training and testing.

We were fortunate enough to have the cooperation and support of the North Carolina State Bureau of Investigation (NCSBI), whose personnel have had much experience in this area. They also had realistic data on which we could test our hypotheses and systems. Researchers in voice recognition know well the value of actually occurring data and how difficult it is to collect. Through the cooperation of NCSBI, much of this work had already been done for us.

Together with the NCSBI experts, we established a classification of tasks which a forensic voice-recognition system should be able to handle.

Forensic Recognition Classification

Type 1: One Unknown and Multiple Known Suspects

This kind of task is similar to closed-set voice recognition, that is, where it is known a priori that the unknown is in a set of known speakers, as discussed in Chapter 1.

One scenario in which this task might arise is as follows: a murder threat spoken in a female voice is left on an answering machine. The telephone call is traced to an office building in which six females are employed. In this situation, the suspects can be recorded on clean channels with multiple recording sessions. The channel for the unknown recording (i.e., the threat) can be determined with some degree of accuracy since the telephone used in the threat can be identified, the likely path through the telephone network can be determined, and, of course, the machine on which the threat was actually recorded is available for analysis.

Type 2: One Unknown and One Suspect

This scenario might arise when a bomb threat is traced to a single-occupant residence. The task is to compare the occupant's voice with the voice in the bomb threat. To determine a recognition score for this type of scenario, a database of impostor reference speakers is necessary. Impostor speakers are known not to have produced the exemplar. The impostors should have the same sex, dialect, and age as the suspect, and the recordings of the database should be of similar quality and length as the recordings of the suspect.

In this scenario, law enforcement agents would have to demonstrate that the speaker of the threat and the suspect are in fact the same person. This would be suggested if the suspect matched the exemplar much better than all the impostors. On the other hand, a suspect could also be exonerated with this type of recognition application. That would occur if the suspect were statistically indistinguishable from the group of impostors.

Type 3: Two Unknowns: Are They of the Same Speaker?

This scenario could arise, for example, during an investigation of drug dealers. Investigators might want to know if the speakers in two separate surveillance tapes were the same person. If both recordings had been made in the same way—say, by a body microphone on an undercover agent—the problem would be less difficult than if the recordings had been made over different or unknown channels. Another common Type 3 application is that of recorded bomb threats made on different occasions: Are they made by the same person?

Type 4: One Unknown and No Suspects

In this scenario, a bomb threat may have been delivered from a public telephone, presenting a difficult problem. The best that law enforcement agents could hope to achieve from a voice-recognition system would be a list of suspects who could be investigated by other means. To perform Type 4 voice recognition and obtain such a list, a very large database of speakers would be necessary. This database could be created in a manner similar to fingerprint databases or photo albums of mug shots.

The voice-recognition system described in this chapter can solve the four tasks listed above with varying degrees of accuracy. When implemented, the system should allow law-enforcement agents to focus a search on possible suspects who have a higher probability of having committed the crime in question.

Since the system is not required to operate in real time, it does not require tremendous amounts of computer speed. The prototype system runs on a PC that, in 1997, could be purchased for under $2,000. A digital signal-processing board might double that cost, which is nonetheless fairly modest in terms of what is generally spent on law-enforcement equipment.

For Types 1 and 2 there may be lengthy training data, possibly collected over several days or even several weeks. This would be acceptable to our system, which has been left to run overnight on more than one occasion. What is important is that our system performs accurately with short *test* utterances, that is, recorded bomb threats and the like. Also important is the fact that the system is capable of performing well on both clean and noisy speech.

IDEAL VOICE RECOGNITION

In this section we will describe ideal voice-recognition systems. The purpose of the discussion is to find the theoretical limits of voice-recognition performance when all the practical restrictions are lifted. For example, ideal systems should be unaffected by:

- Noise;
- Utterance variations, for example fast talking versus slow talking rates;
- Changes in the speaker's emotional state, such as the onset of anger or frustration;
- Changes in the speaker's physical state, such as illness;
- The passage of time, for example the changes in a person's voice as he or she ages;
- Intentional disguises, for example speaking with the nostrils pinched.

While ideal systems should be the ultimate goal of designers of voice-recognition systems, there are practical considerations that make the achievement of this goal difficult. These will also be discussed in this section.

The theoretical limit on the performance of voice-recognition systems is directly related to the uniqueness of voices among the members of the human race. The uniqueness of an individual's voice is a consequence of both the physical features of the person's vocal tract and the person's mental ability to control the muscles in the vocal tract. The physical features of an individual's vocal tract consist of the overall length of the tract, the height and width of the tract at different positions, and the size and shape of the tongue, teeth, and lips. The density of the tissue in the vocal tract also affects the sounds that the individual can produce. The physical dimensions of an individual's vocal tract determine the range of *possible* sounds that can be made. It is not easy for an individual to change voluntarily these physical characteristics. However, they may change somewhat with aging.

A person's mental ability to control vocal-tract muscles during utterances is learned during childhood. These habits affect the range of sounds that may be *effectively* produced by an individual. The range of sounds is a subset of the set of possible sounds that an individual could create with his or her personal vocal tract. For example, a native speaker of English can learn to pronounce the front rounded vowel of French *lune,* but that is not a sound normally produced by English speakers.

For the most part, the thought process used for controlling the vocal tract is subconscious. During normal conversation, speakers are more concerned with the linguistic content of their speech than with the details of muscle movements within the vocal tract. However, some (but not all) the movements may be altered when an individual disguises his or her voice. Furthermore, new movements of the vocal-tract muscles can be acquired when a speaker learns a new language or dialect.

The transient properties of a person's speech represent the manner in which features such as pitch or formant frequencies change over time during a speech utterance. These properties are another artifact of speakers' mental ability to control their vocal tract. When humans perform voice recognition, they rely heavily on transient properties of the speech signal. This process works well in most cases; however, humans who use this technique can be easily deceived by mimics who mainly imitate the transient properties of a speaker.

Therefore, an ideal voice-recognition system would use only physical features to characterize speakers, since these features cannot be easily changed. However, it is obvious that investigators cannot simply measure the vocal-tract length of an unknown speaker. Thus, numerical values for physical features or parameters would have to be derived from digital signal processing (DSP) parameters extracted from the speech signal, to which investigators do have access.

Some DSP parameters are as follows:

- Frequency ranges of formants;
- LPC coefficients;

- Cepstral coefficients;
- Pitch;
- Spectral moments.

Some physical parameters are as follows:

- Vocal-tract length, width, and breadth;
- Size of tongue;
- Size of teeth;
- Tissue density.

Using this strategy, a comparison of voices can be carried out as follows: The physical parameters of known speakers are determined either by following the process shown in Figure 3.1 or by using physical measuring devices and X-ray or MRI imaging. The physical parameters of an unknown speaker could be approximated from the speech signal using the process shown in Figure 3.1. Those physical parameters would then be compared with the physical parameters of the known speakers. The known speaker with the closest matching set of physical parameters would be declared the best choice for the identity of the unknown speaker. A confidence value for the decision could be determined based on the variances of the estimated parameters.

An ideal system would also be able to compensate for the common changes of physical parameters due to aging of the speaker or temporary changes in physical condition due to illness or stress.

Since many independent, continuously valued physical parameters of the vocal tract exist, it is unlikely that two

Figure 3.1 Ideal parameter extraction.

speakers, even if they sounded very similar to each other, would have the same values for all parameters. Suppose that vocal tracts could be effectively represented by 15 independent physical features, with each feature taking on one of 10 discrete values. If the vocal tract could be modeled that accurately, then 10^{15} individuals in the population could be distinguished.

Unfortunately, because of the complexity of speech signals, researchers have not been able perform the second transformation—from DSP parameters to physical parameters—with the accuracy necessary for speaker recognition. In Chapter 5, we will discuss some possible methods for solving this problem directly. As a compromise, the DSP parameters themselves are currently used in nonideal voice-recognition systems.

Another approach to ideal voice recognition exists that does not require the use of physical parameters. Earlier, we stated that the physical parameters determined the range of possible sounds. Instead of modeling speakers by the actual physical parameters of their vocal tracts, speakers can be modeled by the range of sounds made possible by those parameters. These ranges may be viewed either as fuzzy sets or by sets of values satisfying systems of constraints. If the ranges of sounds are viewed as sets, then multidimensional volumes in a parameter space may be used for modeling them. Figures 3.2 and 3.3 suggest how the modeling would be accomplished. The intersection of sets indicates that the same sound can be produced by individuals in both sets. For example, the area of human sounds that intersects the set of canine sounds is probably not very large.[1] With higher numbers of independent dimensions of the parameter space, the amount of intersection between sets will diminish.

Figure 3.3 suggests the way in which these parameter spaces of sounds could be used for implementing a voice-

---

1. In fuzzy terms, contains members most of which have a low coefficient of membership.

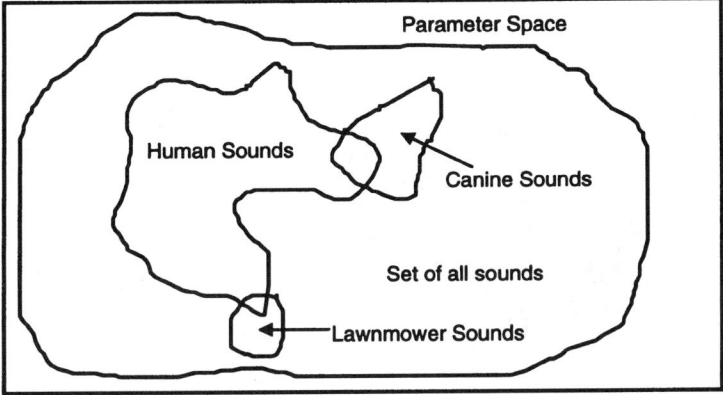

Figure 3.2 Set of all sounds.

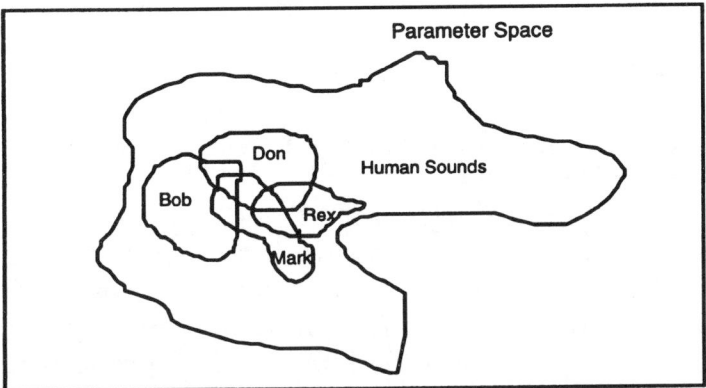

Figure 3.3 Set of human sounds.

recognition system. First, a set of feature vectors would be obtained from the unknown speaker. If a large number of those feature vectors were located in regions of the parameter space that were unique to a known speaker, such as the shaded region in Figure 3.4, then the owner of the shaded region would be the best choice for the identity of the unknown speaker. VQ voice-recognition systems work on this principle (see Chapter 2). However, they perform only a crude

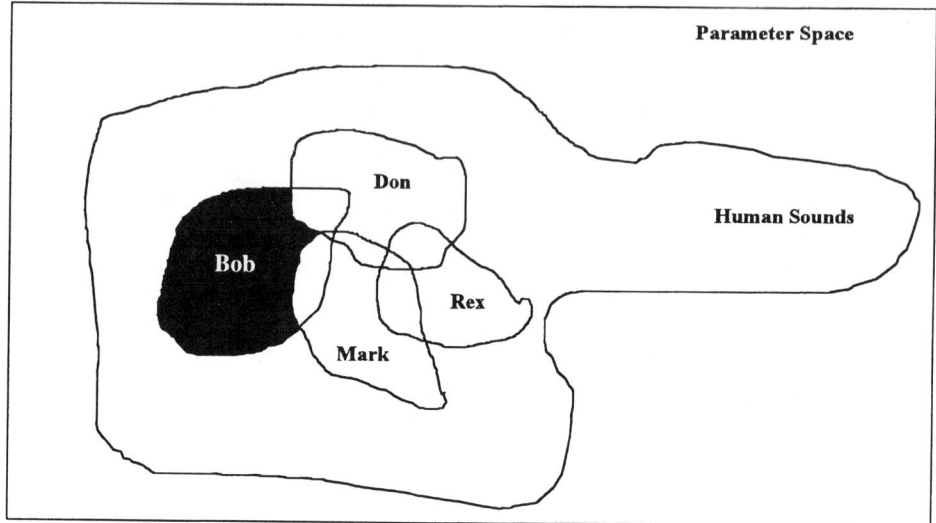

Figure 3.4 Unique area of parameter space.

approximation of the idealized multidimensional fuzzy sets suggested in Figure 3.4.

In a preliminary experiment, we attempted to build a system that would actually determine the fuzzy sets for each speaker. The parameter space consisted of the center frequencies of the lowest formants. Fuzzy membership values for each speaker were determined by creating normalized multidimensional histograms based on the number of occurrences of each formant n-tuple. An example of a two-parameter set is shown in Figure 3.5.

Alternatively, if speakers are modeled as systems of constraints, then each feature vector from a speaker is a valid solution to a set of constraints. A hypothetical constraint might be as follows:

$$c_1 f_1 + c_2(f_2 - f_1) + c_3 f_3 = c_4 + c_5 f_0 \qquad (3.1)$$

where c_i's are constants, f_0 is the pitch, and f_1, f_2, and f_3 are formant frequencies. The goal would be to determine the set

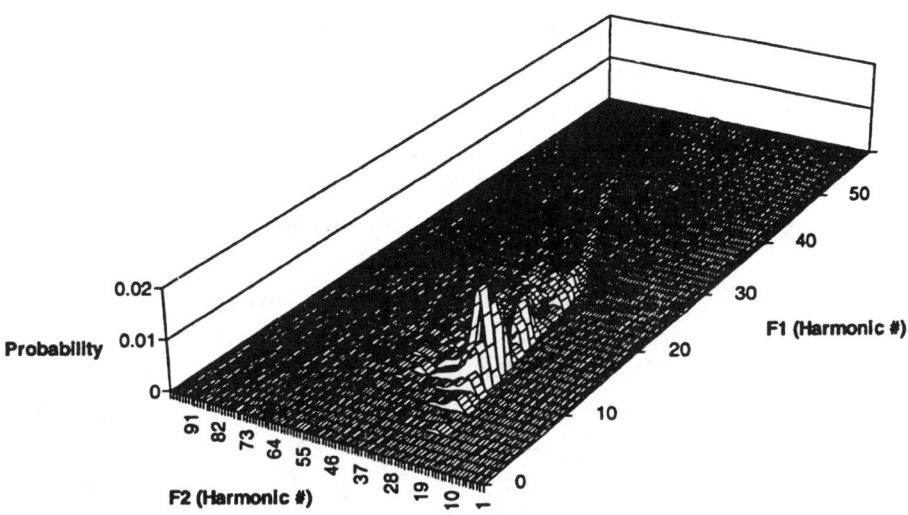

Figure 3.5 Fuzzy set of speaker (two formants).

of constraints that would allow only the feature vectors from the speaker being modeled to be valid. Thus, the constant values in the constraints would be roughly equivalent to the physical parameters of the speaker's vocal tract but would not necessarily be mapped onto any specific physical parameter. This method is similar to the way in which artificial neural networks have been used to perform voice recognition. The constants, c_i's, are simply the weights in the neural network.

There are several problems with trying to model speaker vocal tracts by the ranges of possible sounds that the speaker can produce. First, any model built using this strategy would be sensitive to utterance variation. Thus, long training and test utterances would be needed. Second, the regions for different speakers are very likely to overlap unless the set of parameters is chosen with great care.

These deficiencies led us to a design strategy that we used for the system presented here. The following section will be devoted to describing the system in detail.

A SEGREGATING VOICE-RECOGNITION SYSTEM

To implement a voice-recognition system that would strive for ideal performance, we used a segregating approach. Many of the concepts underlying our system are adaptations of some of the ideas of fuzzy set-based recognition.

As stated earlier, fuzzy set recognition works by finding areas of parameter space that are dominated by vectors from one speaker—that is, space in which the fuzzy set coefficients of membership are highest for the one speaker. These areas are called *global areas of uniqueness.* Determining where these areas are located would require a search of the entire parameter space, a task we would like to avoid since we do not even know all the appropriate parameters for modeling voices of speakers. Even if the appropriate parameter space were known, it would be impossible to determine the exact fuzzy set for representing a person if the training or test utterances were short. Specifically, if the utterances do not contain a wide variety sounds, then there will be gaps in the fuzzy sets that represent that speaker's voice.

For example, in Figure 3.6, the gray area of the parameter space represents the sets of sound produced by speaker "Bob" during the testing phase. This gray area is only a subset of Bob's actual range of sounds. Thus, the actual area of uniqueness in the parameter space is reduced, making the search problem more difficult. The unique areas that do exist in this nonideal parameter space are most likely to be located near sounds common to other individuals in the population, since different speakers make approximately the same sound for each vowel. These areas are called *local areas of uniqueness,* since they are local to each vowel in the language.

Segregation allows local areas of uniqueness to be found more easily than searching the entire parameter space. If performed in a speaker-independent manner, segregation will tend to find areas in the parameter space where speakers *do* overlap—that is, it will find the locations of common sounds,

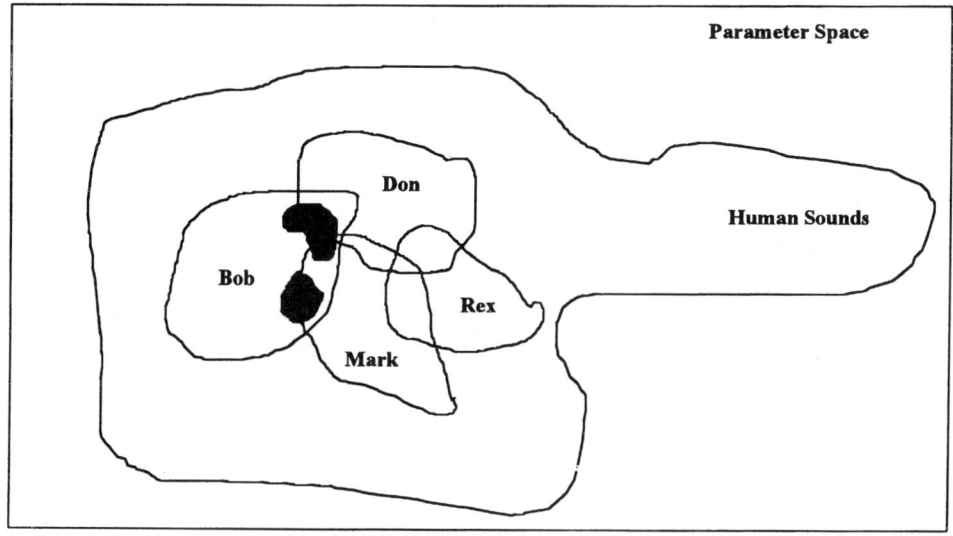

Figure 3.6 Nonideal fuzzy sets.

such as vowels. However, if a second set of more refined features is used for comparisons within each category, then local areas of uniqueness for each speaker can be found. This refinement will reduce the amount of training and test data required to find areas of the parameter space that are unique to each individual. By combining the results from several categories, one can achieve high accuracy.

This entire process is analogous to comparing two photographs by zooming in on several areas of each and then determining the minute differences or similarities in each expanded area. For example, imagine that you are given the task of determining if the persons depicted in two photographs are the same individual. You might first compare the noses of the two individuals. Certain characteristics of the photographs would allow you first to locate the nose in both photographs. With the aid of a magnifying glass, you could then examine the fine structure of each individual's nose to determine its color, shape, and other qualities. If the fine structures of the noses in both photographs were similar, you could say that the two photographs represented individuals with similar noses.

At this point, you might be somewhat confident that the photographs depicted the same individual. If this process were repeated for other facial objects, such as eyes, mouth, and ears, with similar results, then that confidence would rise with each facial object examined. If you were able to detect a similarity between all the facial objects displayed in the photographs, then the probability that the two photographs depicted the same individual would become very high.

Our methods for performing automated speaker recognition operate in a similar fashion. Instead of using coarse facial objects such as nose, eyes, and mouth as areas on which to zoom in, our algorithm uses areas of a coarse feature space defined by the lowest three formants. To describe the fine structure of the object being zoomed in on, the algorithm uses the highly detailed inverse filter spectral coefficients.

A segregating system first separates input feature vectors into categories (segregation) and then compares feature vectors within each category with other feature vectors within the same category (comparison). Each category is equivalent to a facial object in the analogy presented above—that is, nose, mouth, or ear. Each feature vector within a category is equivalent to one partial description of that facial object.

As mentioned in Chapter 2, several segregating approaches for voice recognition have been discussed in the literature. However, none of these systems uses the distinction of coarse parameters for segregation and fine parameters for comparison. They simply use the same features for segregation and comparison. Wang describes a system in which feature vectors are segregated using VQ and features in each category are weighted by the variance within that category [1]. Savic presents a system that uses ergotic HMMs for segregating feature vectors [2]. Each state in the HMM represents a different broad phonetic category. In Savic's system, a Bayesian classifier is used for determining the identity of vectors in each category. Matsui describes a similar system, in which HMMs are used for segregation and VQ is used within each category [3]. Thus, each known speaker is represented by several codebooks, one for each category.

The coarse/fine approach presented here requires an increase in computation time and storage requirements. However, for forensic use, these penalties are not significant, since the processing takes place off line.

The present system contains other distinctions as well. For example, the feature vectors it uses for comparison are much larger than those used by voice-recognition systems reported in the literature. The inverse filter spectral coefficients will contain some undesirable information, such as random noise and spectral lines. However, there is no information loss from the original signal as there is with LPC and cepstral techniques. Moreover, long-term averaging of the spectral coefficients in a segregating system will be able to filter out irrelevant information without losing the pertinent fine structure of the spectral envelope. This fine structure is the key to performing high accuracy voice recognition with large populations of speakers.

Another characteristic of the system is the use of information only from voiced segments of utterances. Since vowels contain the most energy of an utterance, they will have higher signal-to-noise ratios (SNRs). Also, the formants found in vowels contain more information about the size and shape of the speaker's vocal tract then consonants do.

Finally, we use a novel distance measure for comparing vectors within each category and introduce new methods for combining the distortion measures from several categories. These novel aspects of the system will be described in further detail in subsequent sections.

System Tasks

The system performs the following tasks: feature extraction, vector segregation, and comparison of reference vectors within each category (Figure 3.7). These steps will be detailed.

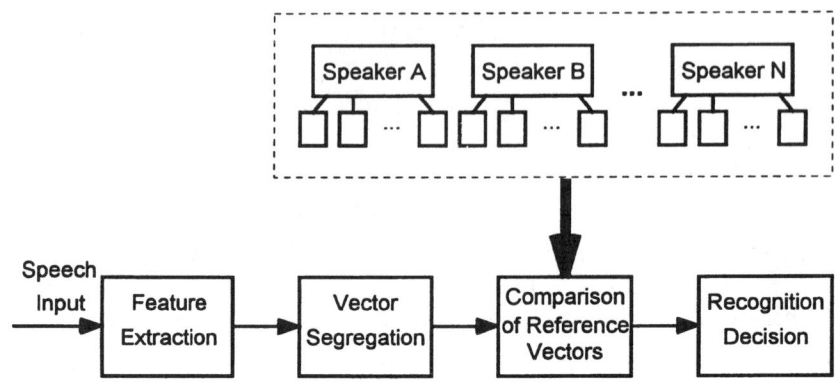

Figure 3.7 Voice-recognition procedure.

Feature Extraction

Input speech is sampled at 16 kHz with 14 bits of resolution. These settings provide enough frequency and dynamic range to represent human speech accurately, since most information in human speech is to be found in spectral bands less than 8 kHz.

The speech is processed in 16 ms segments, or windows. This relatively long window permits high-resolution frequency measurements using a 256 point FFT. The 16 ms windows of speech are processed at 4-ms intervals, so adjacent windows overlap by 12 ms. Thus, each window is correlated with the adjacent windows but independent enough to make the calculation worth performing.

Calulate Zero Crossing Rate and Pitch Peak. For each window of speech, a voiced/unvoiced decision is made based on the zero crossing rate and the height of the pitch peak in the autocorrelation function. Waveforms from voiced and unvoiced segments of speech are shown in Figures 3.8 and 3.9.

The zero crossing rate is the count of the number of times the waveform crosses the x-axis within the specified window of time. Unvoiced windows will have a higher zero crossing

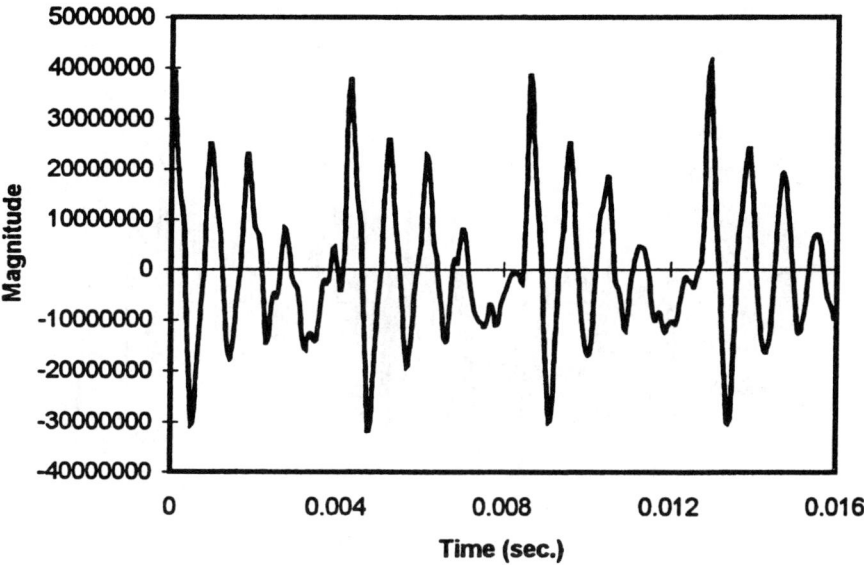

Figure 3.8 Example of a voiced segment of speech from the TIMIT Database.

rate than voiced segments. The zero crossing rate for voiced waveform in Figure 3.8 is 33, and the zero crossing rate for unvoiced waveform in Figure 3.9 is 74. Speech segments with zero crossing rates higher than 70 are considered to be unvoiced. This value was determined by trial and error.

A weighted auto-correlation function is used for determining if the signal is periodic. The auto-correlation function is defined as follows:

$$ACF_n = \sum_{m=n}^{N} S_m S_{m-n} \tag{3.2}$$

where ACF_n is the nth auto-correlation function value, S_n is the nth sample in the signal, and N is the number of samples in the window. The weighting function is:

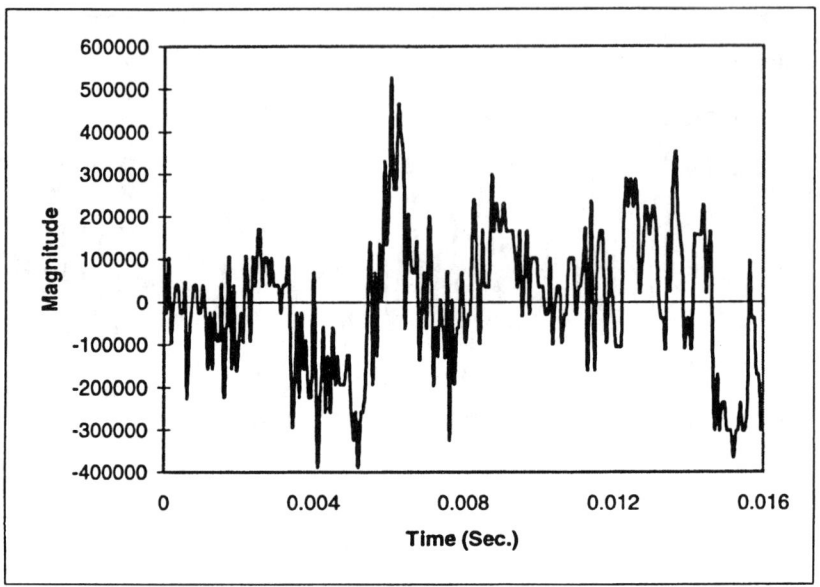

Figure 3.9 Example of an unvoiced segment of speech from the TIMIT Database.

$$WACF_n = \left[4 + 4\left(\frac{n - pitch\_period\_minimum}{N - pitch\_period\_minimum}\right)\right]ACF_n$$

(3.3)

where $WACF_n$ is the nth weighted auto-correlation function value. The weighting function accentuates the peak in the auto-correlation function. A large peak in the weighted auto-correlation function indicates that the signal is periodic; thus, it was probably voiced. The peak in the WACF at sample zero is not considered since all waveforms will have a peak at this position. The value of this peak is directly related to the energy of the segment but not its periodicity. Any peaks at non-zero positions must be greater than the peak at position zero for the segment to be considered voiced.

The weighted auto-correlation functions for the speech segments in Figures 3.8 and 3.9 are shown in Figures 3.10 and 3.11.

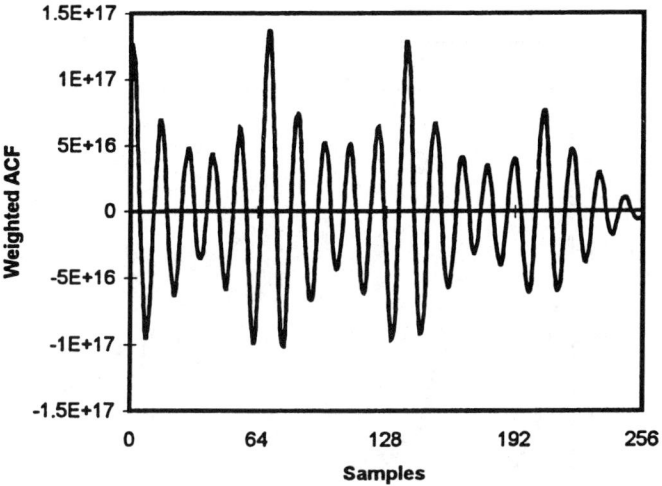

Figure 3.10 Weighted auto-correlation function for voiced segment of speech.

At this point in the processing, the unvoiced segments of speech are discarded.

Windowing and Preemphasis. The following Hamming function is applied to the remaining segments of speech to minimize edge effects in subsequent processing:

$$w_n = 1.5863(0.54 - 0.46\cos(2\pi(n)/256) \qquad (3.4)$$

where w_n is the nth point in the function (see Figure 3.12). At each sample point in the segment of speech, the speech signal value is multiplied by the function value as shown in (3.5):

$$S'_n = w_n S_n \qquad (3.5)$$

where S_n is a sample from the original signal and S'_n is the signal after the Hamming function is applied.

The window of speech is then preemphasized with the following filter:

$$S''_n = S'_n + 0.95(S'_{n-1}) \qquad (3.6)$$

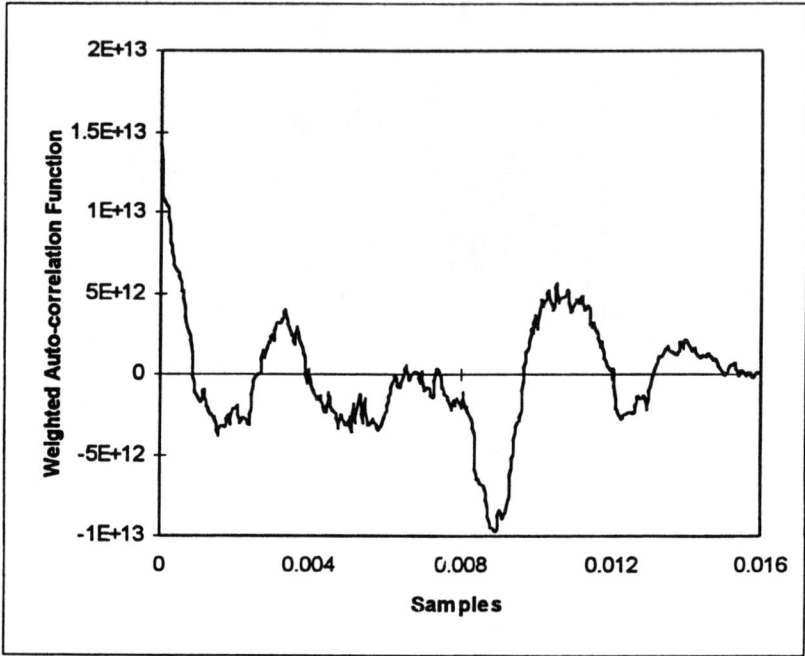

Figure 3.11 Weighted auto-correlation function for unvoiced segment of speech.

where S_n' is a sample from the previous step and S_n'' is the preemphasized signal. Preemphasis is used to amplify the higher-frequency spectrum (see Figure 3.13).

Calculate LPC Spectrum. The LPC-derived spectrum is used for determining the center frequencies of the lowest three formants using a simple peak-finding algorithm.

Calculate Formant Frequencies. The peak-finding algorithm would identify peaks (formants) at the 18th, 51st, and 69th harmonics (1125 Hz, 3187 Hz, and 4312 Hz). (See Figure 3.14).

Calculate Inverse Spectral Coefficients. Then, 128 normalized inverse filter spectral coefficients are calculated using an FFT algorithm (see Figure 3.15).

Methods of Context-Free Voice Recognition 81

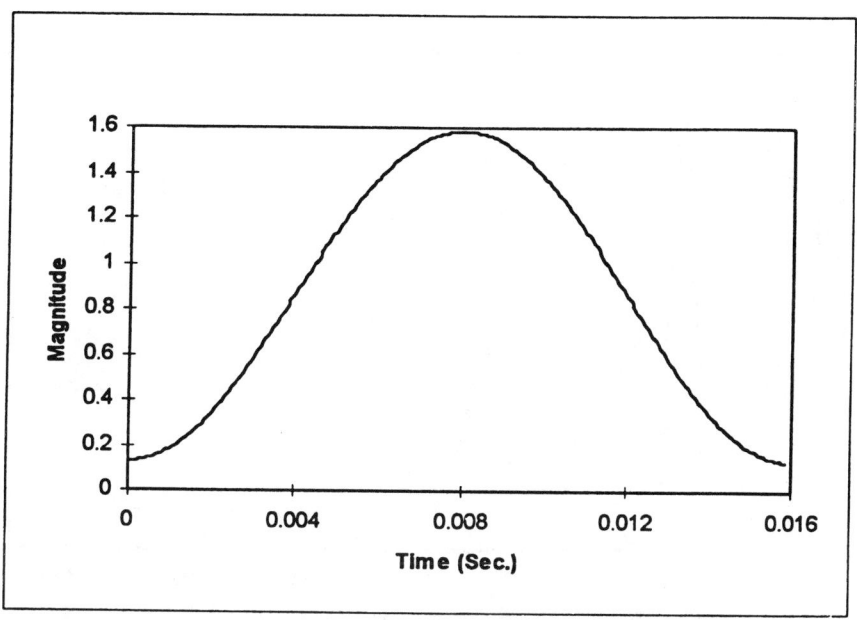

Figure 3.12 The Hamming window used.

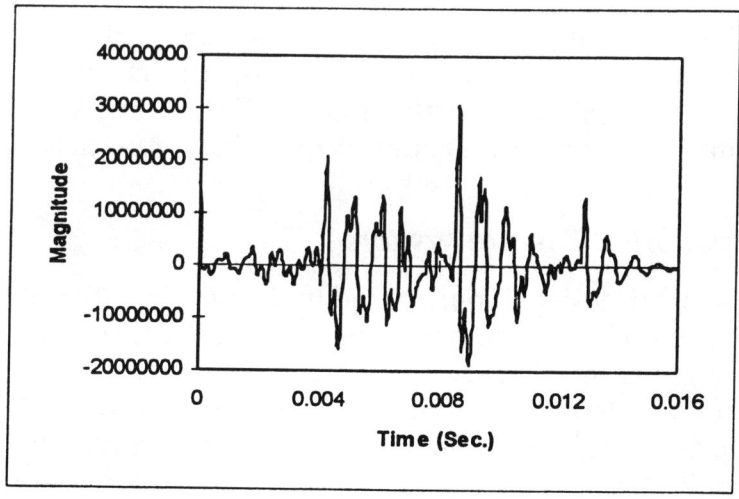

Figure 3.13 Speech segment after the Hamming function and preemphasis have been applied.

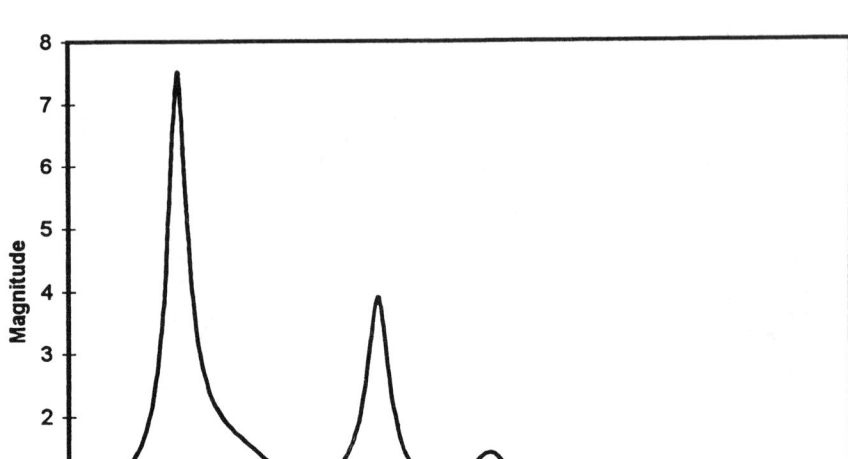

Figure 3.14 LPC of window of speech.

The output for this window of speech would be a feature vector containing the three formant positions and the 128 inverse filter spectral coefficients (IFSCs) (Figure 3.16).

The entire process is summarized in Figure 3.17.

Segregation of Feature Vectors

The segregation step is performed by using VQ with one codebook of size 16. It is trained using the Linde, Gray, and Buzo (LGB) algorithm [4] with just the formant frequency components of the feature vectors as input. Each vector in this generic codebook represents the centroid of a category, where the parameter space is defined by the center frequencies of the lowest three formants. Since the purpose of the segregation step is to find areas of the parameter space where speakers overlap, the same codebook is used for all speakers. Thus, to

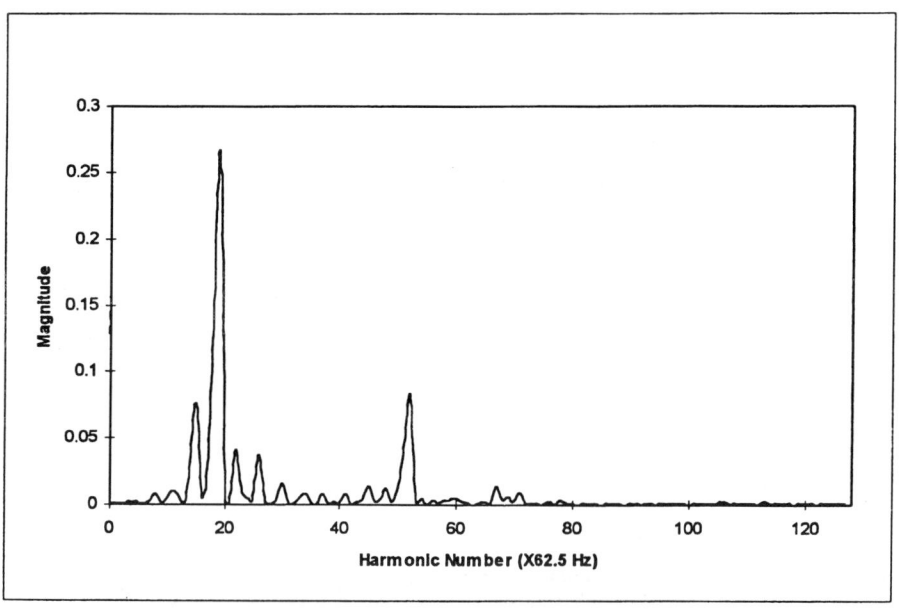

Figure 3.15 Inverse filter spectral coefficients.

F_1	F_2	F_3	$IFSC_1$	...	$IFSC_{128}$
18	51	69	0.000451	...	0.000845

Figure 3.16 The feature vector.

find these areas, a large set of training vectors is taken randomly from several male and female speakers. VQ is performed on this set of data to create the generic codebook. This time-consuming process needs only to be performed once when creating the voice-recognition system. The values of the centroids for the generic codebook are shown in Table 3.1.

After a set of feature vectors has been collected for a speaker during training or testing, the generic codebook is used for segregating the vectors into 16 categories, which is adequate for distinguishing most English vowels. Each vector

84   Voice Recognition

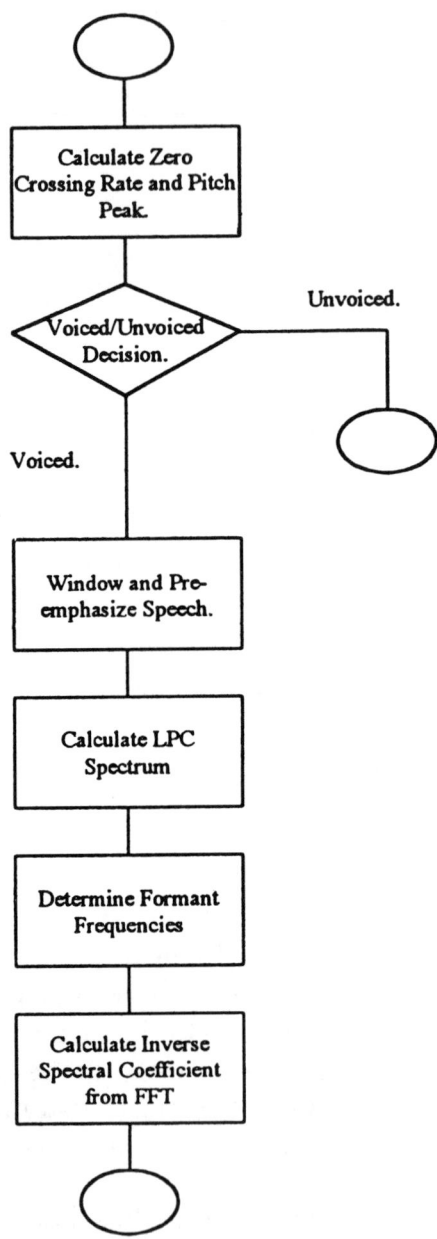

Figure 3.17   The feature-extraction process.

Table 3.1
Generic Codebook Centroids

Vector Number	Formant Harmonic Position		
	F_1	F_2	F_3
1	8.944099	19.03727	34.95186
2	8.080953	22.36667	76.70000
3	7.966513	20.23903	52.00116
4	8.191176	20.73529	102.38240
5	7.812065	25.48376	39.39791
6	6.814286	48.46000	65.17429
7	7.845538	39.07208	49.80893
8	7.536364	44.54546	102.56360
9	9.141453	18.17474	42.98714
10	5.820197	39.48030	76.06651
11	7.087467	23.98042	60.58094
12	7.848485	28.51515	119.16670
13	6.505085	31.37966	43.17797
14	7.693548	56.03764	81.29570
15	6.460187	38.54216	59.65925
16	7.450000	59.53333	116.78330

is placed in a category based on the closest centroid in the codebook. Distance is calculated using the Euclidean distance between the vectors of formant frequencies.

For example, the category for a voiced segment of speech can be determined as follows. Suppose the vector to classify is:

$$v = \{18, 51, 69\}$$

The distance between the vector and the centroid of the first category is:

$$D_1 = \sqrt{(18 - 8.944)^2 + (51 - 19.037)^2 + (69 - 34.952)^2} \quad (3.7)$$
$$D_1 = 59.528$$

The distances between the vector to classify and the remaining vectors in the codebook are shown in Table 3.2.

From Table 3.2, we see that the example vector belongs in category 1.

Since the formant frequencies are not needed after segregation, they may be discarded, leaving just the 128 inverse spectral coefficients in each feature vector. This new vector would be added to the current set of vectors in the Category 1 data file. This process is repeated for all the input vectors for a speaker.

After all the input vectors have been put into categories, the estimated mean and variance vectors and the number of vectors in each of the 16 categories are determined from that category's set of feature vectors. After this step is performed for each category, the original feature vectors can be discarded and the model of a speaker is complete.

Table 3.2
Distance to Each Centroid

Vector Number	Distance
1	59.52792
2	81.10769
3	69.01933
4	90.93582
5	64.48833
6	84.20892
7	74.63720
8	97.38770
9	63.69906
10	85.83034
11	74.36841
12	99.08605
13	68.53272
14	92.76749
15	78.73006
16	105.96390

The mean and variance vectors can be stored in arrays of 128 floating point values and the count can be stored in an integer value. Thus, the total amount of memory required to store the model of the speaker is:

Memory = (Number of Categories) ·
(mean vector + variance vector + count)
Memory = 16 · ((128 · fp) + (128 · fp) + (1 · int))
Memory = 4096 · fp + 16 · int

where fp is the size of a floating point value and int is the size of an integer value.

Comparison of Vectors Within Categories

To compare two speaker models (known versus unknown), comparisons must be made within each category of feature vectors. The results of these comparisons are distortion values that are combined to form a total distortion measure between the speaker models.

The following computation is performed for each category of feature vectors:

$$d_j = \frac{1}{n} \sum_{i=1}^{n} t_{i,j} \frac{|u_{i,j} - k_{i,j}|}{(u_{i,j} + k_{i,j})}, \ 1 \leq j \leq 16, \ 1 \leq i \leq 128 = n \quad (3.8)$$

where d_j is the distortion score for the jth category, n is the number of components in the feature vector (i.e., 128), $u_{i,j}$ is the value of the ith component of the mean vector in the jth category for the unknown speaker, and $k_{i,j}$ is the value of the ith component of the mean vector in the jth category for the known speaker.

The weighting factor, $t_{i,j}$, is the confidence in rejecting the hypothesis that the means of the ith component from the known and unknown speakers are equal. (See below for precise definition.) This calculation assumes that the variances of the ith components from both speakers are unknown and not equal. A lookup table of Student's T-scores is used in the following manner [5]:

1. Assume the following definitions:
    $n_{j,x}$ = Number of samples in category j for the first speaker.

    $n_{j,y}$ = Number of samples in category j for the second speaker.

    $\bar{x}_{i,j}$ = The estimated mean of the ith component for the first speaker in the jth category, where

    $$\bar{x}_{i,j} = \frac{1}{n_{j,x}} \sum_{l=1}^{n_{j,x}} u_{i,j,l}, \text{ when } u_{i,j,l} \text{ is the } i\text{th component}$$

    in the jth category for the lth vector from the first speaker.

    $\bar{y}_{i,j}$ = The estimated mean of the ith component for the second speaker in the jth category, where

    $$\bar{y}_{i,j} = \frac{1}{n_{j,y}} \sum_{l=1}^{n_{j,y}} k_{i,j,l}, \text{ when } k_{i,j,l} \text{ is the } i\text{th component in}$$

    the jth category for the lth vector from the second speaker.

    $s_{j,x}$ = The estimated variance of the ith component for the first speaker, where

    $$s_{j,x} = \frac{1}{n_{j,x} - 1} \sum_{l=1}^{n_{j,x}} (u_{i,j,l} - \bar{x}_{i,j})^2$$

    $s_{j,y}$ = The estimated variance of the ith component for the second speaker, where

    $$s_{j,y} = \frac{1}{n_{j,y} - 1} \sum_{l=1}^{n_{j,y}} (k_{i,j,l} - \bar{y}_{i,j})^2$$

2. The number of degrees of freedom is the closest integer to:

$$v_j = -2 + \frac{\left(\dfrac{s_{j,x}^2}{n_{j,x}} + \dfrac{s_{j,y}^2}{n_{j,y}}\right)^2}{\dfrac{\left(\dfrac{s_{j,x}^2}{n_{j,x}}\right)^2}{n_{j,x}+1} + \dfrac{\left(\dfrac{s_{j,y}^2}{n_{j,y}}\right)^2}{n_{j,y}+1}} \qquad (3.9)$$

3. The test statistic is defined as:

$$t_j = \frac{\bar{x}_j - \bar{y}_j}{\sqrt{\dfrac{s_{j,x}^2}{n_{j,x}} + \dfrac{s_{j,y}^2}{n_{j,y}}}} \qquad (3.10)$$

4. A lookup table is used for determining the confidence in rejecting the hypothesis. The critical region occurs when $|t_j| > t_{\alpha;v_j}$, where $t_{\alpha;v_j}$ is the value given by a lookup table that contains the approximate value of $t_{\alpha;v_j}$ for different values of α and v_j, where $\alpha \in \{0.0, 0.6, 0.75. 0.90, 0.95. 0.975, 0.99, 0.995\}$ and $v_j \in \{10, 20, 30, 40, 60, 120, 32000\}$. Linear interpolation is used to estimate the value of α where $|t| = t_{\alpha;v_j}$. The weighting factor, $t_{i,j}$, is equal to α.

The weighting factor, which has a range of 0.0 to 1.0, gives more emphasis to features that are believed to contain more information for differentiating the two speakers.

The distance measure in (3) is normalized by the sum of the signal values at each point in the FFT spectrum. This normalization prevents errors in the magnitude of formant peaks from dominating the distortion measure. This normalization is another unique feature of the system described here. A graph displaying typical average category vectors from two speakers is shown in Figure 3.18.

A final score for each comparison is determined by a weighted summation of the scores for each category:

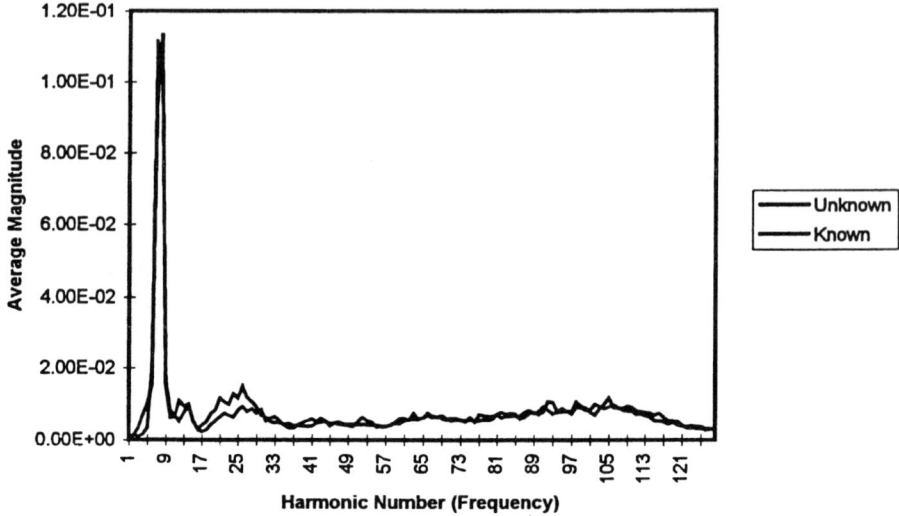

Figure 3.18 Comparison of category vectors.

$$D = \frac{1}{n}\sum_{j=1}^{n} w_j d_j \qquad (3.11)$$

where w_j is the weight for the jth category, d_j is the distortion of the jth category, and n is the number of categories actually used. A category is used if the model of any member of the target population contains enough vectors in that category to exceed a threshold value. The threshold cutoff prevents outliers in the data from skewing distortion measures. The threshold is currently set at 5.

The category weighting factor, w_j, is determined in a speaker-independent manner. Two sets of distortion scores for each category are collected: scores from comparisons in which it is known a priori that the two speakers are the same and scores from comparisons in which it is known a priori that the two speakers are different. The average category distortion values are calculated for each set. The weighting factor for each category is the ratio of the two averages:

$$w_j = \frac{\overline{d}_{diff,j}}{\overline{d}_{same,j}}, \ 1 \leq j \leq 16 \qquad (3.12)$$

where w_j is the weighting factor for the jth category, $\overline{d}_{same,j}$ is the average of the distortion scores for the jth category in comparisons where the speakers are the same, and $\overline{d}_{diff,j}$ is the average of the distortion scores for the jth category in comparisons where the speakers are different.

In comparisons where the length of the test utterance is short, categories may contain no entries for some known speakers while containing valid data for the rest of the population. This phenomenon may be termed the *absence of evidence problem.* If not compensated for, the absence of evidence problem can cause the distortion measures for models with empty categories to be much lower than the rest of the population. To counteract this problem, a penalty equal to the average distortion value for the category is added to the distortion measure for models with empty categories.

Recognition Decisions

For speaker identification, the model of the unknown is compared with the models of all known speakers. The best match is determined by taking the known speaker with the lowest total score. To determine how close a match is, the total score for a member of the population can be placed on a normal distribution scale. The normal distribution scale will yield a number between 0.0 and 1.0 for each member of the population. Scores near 0.5 will be close to the average for the population. A score near 1.0 indicates that the match is much better than others in the population.

An alternative to normalized scores for closed-set identification is the use of binary tree searches. The use of this technique for automatic speaker identification was proposed by Rudasi and Zahorian [6]. When a binary tree search is used, classification is carried out as a series of classifications that involve only two speakers at a time. This approach requires a series of elimination rounds similar to tournaments in sporting events. The winners of each round go on to the next round of competition until only one winner is left. If classification is performed correctly at each comparison, then the tournament winner will be the correct match (Figure 3.19).

Classification is a much easier task if only two speakers are involved. Weights can be fine-tuned to emphasize only the features that are useful for distinguishing the two speakers. Thus, the irrelevant parts of the spectrum can be ignored. These weights will be much different from weights optimized for distinguishing the entire population.

If neither of the two known speakers in a classification is actually the unknown, then the result of the classification is inconsequential, as suggested in Figure 3.20.

The system must achieve correct results only in the comparisons in which one of the two involved speakers is actually the unknown. This fact is reflected in the testing procedures for the system when binary tree search is used.

For speaker verification, normalized scores are used, as binary tree search is inappropriate. Since the distortion scores

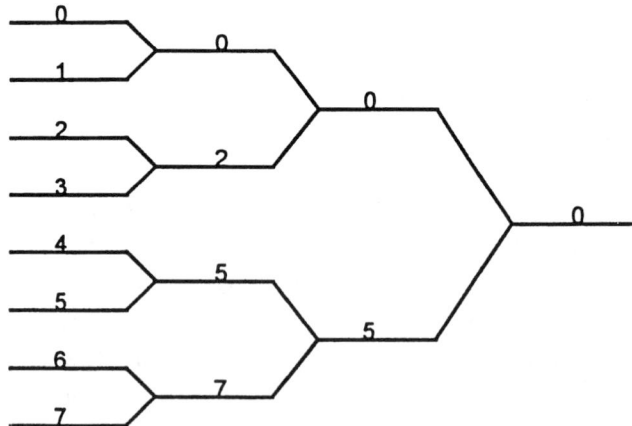

Figure 3.19 Binary tree search tournament.

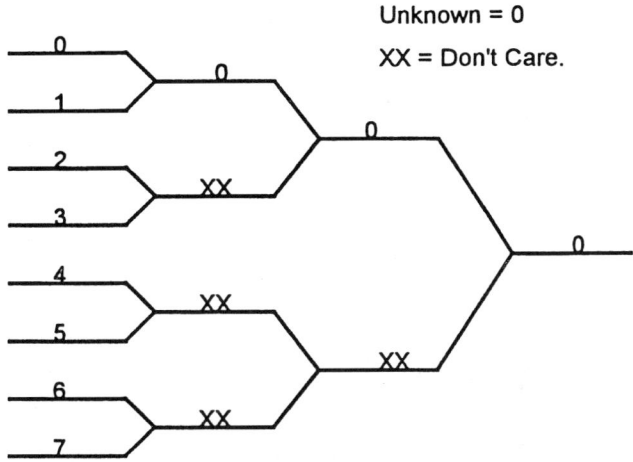

Figure 3.20 Search tree with "don't cares."

for any comparison of two models is affected by the models themselves, a fixed criterion value for accepting or rejecting speakers is not feasible for raw scores. However, the normalized scores have a consistent range of values, which allows the use of a fixed criterion.

To determine a reasonable criterion value, the equal error rate is calculated. The equal error rate is found by adjusting the criterion value until the false acceptance rate is equal to the false rejection rate. This value must be determined experimentally by collecting the normalized recognition scores for a large number of both accepting and rejecting comparisons. An example of an equal error rate graph is shown is Figure 3.21.

In Figure 3.21, an equal error rate of 4.2% is obtained for a criterion value of 0.933. The criterion value determined from the error rate can then be used in future comparisons in which the expected error rates (both false rejection and false acceptance) will be equal to the equal error rate.

Other ratios of error rates can be determined from Figure 3.21. For example, a false acceptance error rate of 0.5% can

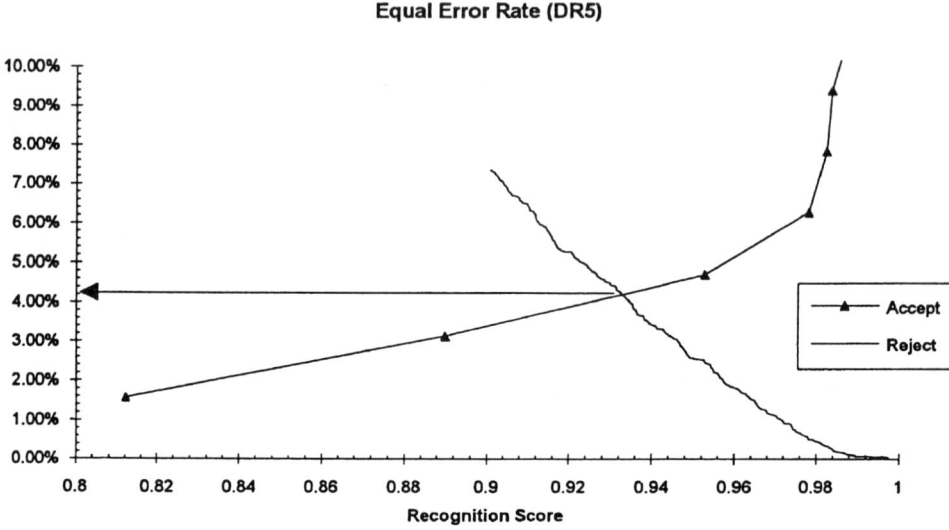

Figure 3.21 Equal error rate.

be achieved with a criterion value of 0.98. With this criterion value, the false rejection rate would be 6.0%.

Channel Variation Compensation

In this section, techniques for compensating for channel variability will be examined. As discussed earlier, there are three major components of channel variation: additive noise, bandpass filtering, and phase distortion. For methods used by our system, only variation in bandpass filtering is a major concern.

Since phase information is not used during any step of signal processing, its variability is not an issue. Furthermore, it is easy to compensate for additive noise. Frequency ranges of the spectrum corrupted by additive noise can simply be discarded. These frequency ranges can be determined from the spectrum of noise during speech-free periods in the recordings. The drawback of this technique is that the number of data points is reduced, which also reduces the accuracy of the system.

The variation of the bandpass filtering of the channel can have major effects on the performance of the system. Bandpass filtering may cause peaks in a speaker's spectrum to be attenuated so that the peaks look more like the peaks of another speaker's unattenuated spectrum. The result of this channel mismatch is very poor recognition performance. Unfortunately, it is difficult to determine the amount of bandpass filtering that is being performed by a channel without knowing the identity of the speaker whose voice is being passed through that channel—but then, the speaker's identity is precisely what is being sought.

Average Filter Compensation Technique

In compensating for channel filtering mismatch, the channel's filter characteristics may be assumed to be stationary; therefore, the average spectrum for all vectors of a given utterance will contain the *true* average spectrum of the speaker attenuated by the stationary filter. (The *true* average spectrum of the speaker is the average spectrum computed for speech recorded on a known nonattenuating channel.) The assumption may not be entirely valid, since variability in the person's voice and in the content of the utterances will cause the *true* average to vary somewhat [7].

For the system described earlier in this chapter, the average spectrum for an utterance can be determined by combining the average vectors for each category weighted by the number of samples for that category. This may be calculated as follows:

$$a_i = \frac{1}{\sum_{j=1}^{16} count_j} \sum_{j=1}^{16} (count_j \cdot k_{i,j}), \quad 1 \le i \le 128 \qquad (3.13)$$

where a_i is the ith component of the average vector for the entire utterance, $k_{i,j}$ is the ith component of the average vector for the jth category, and $count_j$ is the number of vectors in the jth category.

The ratio of the average spectrum for the unknown utterance and the average spectrum of one of the known utterances will indicate the channel filter mismatch between the channel used for recording the unknown and the channel used for recording the known. This ratio is calculated as follows:

$$r_{i,known} = \frac{a_{i,unknown}}{a_{i,known}}, 1 \leq i \leq 128 \qquad (3.14)$$

where $r_{i,known}$ is the channel filter mismatch between the unknown and a specific known speaker at the ith component of the feature vector, $a_{i,unknown}$ is the ith component of the average vector for the entire utterance from the unknown speaker, and $a_{i,known}$ is the ith component of the average vector for the entire utterance from a specific known speaker.

By multiplying this ratio by the average vector for each of the sixteen categories of the known speaker, we can make the filter characteristics of the two channels more similar. This calculation is shown below:

$$k'_{i,j} = r_{i,known} \cdot k_{i,j}, 1 \leq i \leq 128, 1 \leq j \leq 16 \qquad (3.15)$$

where $k'_{i,j}$ is the ith component of the modified average vector for the jth category, and $k_{i,j}$ is the ith component of the original average vector for the jth category. The effects of this transformation are shown graphically in Figure 3.22.

The reshaping of the average spectrum of the known speakers lowers the distortion scores for both the correct speakers and the impostors. Thus, the actual recognition performance is relatively modest. In the experiments reported in Chapter 4, a 10% improvement was achieved using this technique.

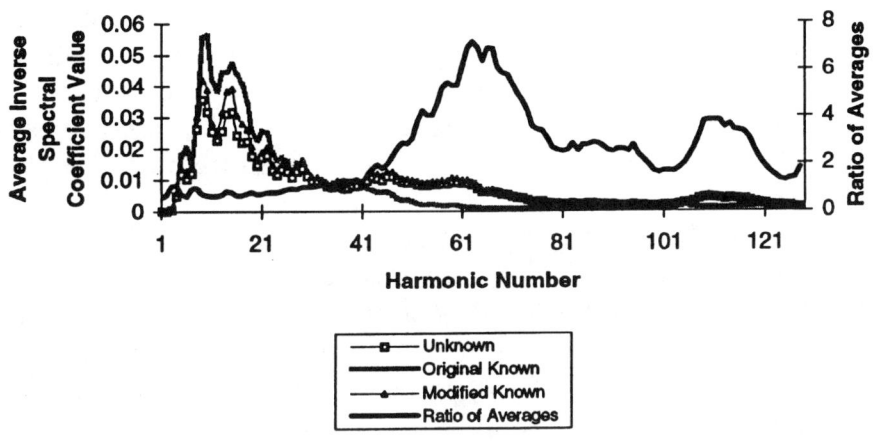

Figure 3.22 Average filter compensation.

Rehumanizing Filter Technique

Since the average filter compensation technique is unable to find a unique solution to a problem that is essentially one equation (the bomb threat) in two unknowns (channel and speaker), we have proposed a technique that tries to "guess" the correct filter, thus eliminating one of the unknowns.

In a typical forensic exemplar, a spoken bomb threat over telephone lines, the telephone call may be traced so that most of the components of the channel can be determined—for example, the telephone used by the caller and the recording device used for recording the threat. The filter characteristics of these two devices may be determined experimentally. Thus, the real unknown part of the channel is the actual connection through the telephone system. This path will vary from call to call even if the source and destination stations are same for each call. However, a reasonably accurate estimation of the filter characteristics can be derived from FCC guidelines for telephone channel performance and from experimental studies.

An estimate of the complete unknown channel may be formed by combining the filter characteristics of these three devices. Thus, the real job in determining the filter characteristics of the unknown channel is simply optimizing the estimated filter. The rehumanizing filter technique performs this optimization.

Imagine the following analogous situation: you are given 10 recordings of what lawn mowers sound like when recorded through known nonattenuating channels (obviously, the lawn mowers are running while the recordings are being made). You are also given the recording of an unknown lawn mower. The recording of the unknown lawn mower has been filtered in such a way that it does not actually sound like a lawn mower anymore. Perhaps it now sounds more like an electric razor. However, assume that the recording is of such good quality that if you knew the inverse of the filter used to create the unknown recording, you could exactly recreate the original signal as shown below:

$$u_{filtered}(t) = f(u(t)) \qquad (3.16)$$
$$u(t) = f^{-1}(f(u(t)))$$

The strategy for determining the inverse filter, since we do not actually know the original filter, is to vary parameters of the inverse filter until the unknown sounds most like a lawn mower, based on comparisons with the known lawn mowers.

This same strategy can be used for human voices instead of lawn mowers. The inverse filter is varied until the unknown sounds most like a human. The test for "sounding most like a human" can be performed by the voice-recognition system itself. When the correct inverse filter is used, the average distortion between the unknown and a population of known speakers will be minimized. This behavior was verified experimentally, and the results of these experiments will be shown in the next chapter. In addition to the minimization of the average distortion, the minimum distortion (the best match) and the standard deviation of the distortion scores are also minimized.

Thus, if an estimate of the channel's filter characteristics can be made by analysis of the individual components of the channel, then the rehumanizing filter technique may be used to determine a more accurate estimate of the channel.

All forensic recordings are of too poor quality for the inverse filtering of the filtered signal to restore the original signal. Thus, some information will be lost by the original filtering, and recognition will be poorer than when both the knowns and unknown are not filtered. However, by filtering the clean unknowns and the clean knowns with the same filter, a theoretical maximum value for the recognition accuracy obtainable by "guessing" the channel's filter characteristics can be determined. These values will be discussed in the next chapter as well.

Since the original filter destroys some information, it is more reasonable to make the knowns sound more like the unknown by filtering the knowns, instead of inverse-filtering the unknown. Still, the voice-recognition system can be used for determining when the best estimate of the filter has been achieved.

In this section, two techniques for compensating for channel mismatch were discussed. The average filter compensation technique has many drawbacks and offers only a minor improvement in recognition performance. The rehumanizing filter technique proposed here is an alternative method that yields a significant improvement in recognition performance.

Software Implementation

The system described here has been implemented as a series of C and C++ programs for an IBM PC-compatible system.

Some of the C/C++ programs use a Motorola 56001 DSP based coprocessor card to calculate FFTs. The system consists of the components listed in Table 3.3.

The data flow of the system is shown in Figure 3.23.

The source code for these programs is available from the authors.

Table 3.3
System Components of Multigranular Segregating Voice Recognition Program

Component	Function
extract	Performs all the feature extraction operations shown in Figure 3.17. Takes 14-bit PCM speech input files and creates an output file containing a series of complete feature vectors—that is, vectors contain three formant frequencies and 128 inverse spectral components. See "Feature Extraction" section in this chapter for details.
vq	Determines the optimal centroids of categories by using the LGB algorithm for vector quantization. The parameter space consists of the frequencies of the lowest three formants. This program takes as input a series of complete feature vectors (created by *extract*) and creates an output file that contains the coordinates of the category centroids. See "Segregation of Feature Vectors" section in this chapter for details.
vqsort	Segregates sets of feature vectors into categories based on the centroids determined by *vq*. It takes as input the coordinates of the category centroids and a set of complete feature vectors to be segregated. The output of *vqsort* is several sets of feature vectors that contain only inverse spectral coefficients. Each set corresponds to a category determined by *vq*. These sets are stored in files named XXX.exp, where XXX is a three-digit category number. See "Segregation of Feature Vectors" section in this chapter for details.
findw	Estimates the mean and variance vectors for the sets of feature vectors created by *vqsort*. The output of *findw* is a set of files, one for each category, each containing the estimated mean and variance for just the inverse filter spectral coefficients, not the formant frequencies. Each file also contains a count of the number of feature vectors in that category. These values are stored in files names XXX.wts, where XXX is a three digit number specifying which category the data belongs to. See "Segregation of Feature Vectors" section in this chapter for details.

Table 3.3 (Continued)

Component	Function
comp	Performs binary comparisons. It can be used in a test mode, where the identity of the unknown is known a priori and all comparisons involving the unknown are performed, or in a run-time mode, where a binary tree search is actually used for speaker identification. *See* the section titled "Comparison of Vectors Within Categories" in this chapter for details.
verf	Performs speaker verification and large population identification. For verification, it can also be used in two modes. In the test mode, each unknown is tested against all known speakers. In run-time mode, the unknown is only tested against the known he/she claims to be. For identification, the program returns the list of distortion scores for each known speaker. *See* the section titled "Comparison of Vectors Within Categories" in this chapter for details.

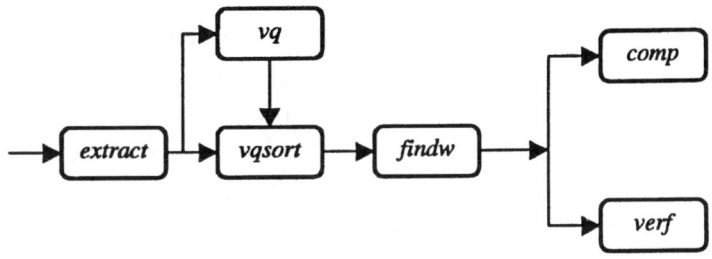

Figure 3.23 Data flow of system.

LOGISTICS OF FORENSIC SPEAKER IDENTIFICATION

A principal goal of the work described here is the development of a voice-recognition system that can actually be used by law-enforcement agencies. As with the design of any computer software or hardware product, the designers must not ignore the requirements, limitations, or preferences of the intended users of the system. In the process of designing the system, we have shared information and ideas with law enforcement agents at the NCSBI. From these discussions, it is clear that more communication in both directions is needed.

Voice-recognition system designers need to explain to law enforcement agencies the limitations of current voice-recognition technology and discuss what changes are necessary in law-enforcement procedures to increase the effectiveness and applicability of such systems. On the other hand, voice-recognition system designers need to know more about the environment in which their systems would be used. They may achieve this by meeting with a variety of law enforcement agencies and assessing the current state of affairs in regard to voice crimes.

Many steps are required to reach these goals. A few of the preliminary steps and guidelines will be presented in this section.

The first step is to acknowledge the different types of forensic speaker-identification tasks. This taxonomy was given earlier in the chapter and is recapitulated in an abridged form below. This terminology, or something equivalent, needs to be used by both law enforcement agents and voice-recognition experts to ensure proper communication of ideas.

A taxonomy of forensic speaker-recognition tasks should include the elements listed in Table 3.4.

Next, procedures for obtaining exemplars from suspects (knowns) must be refined to ensure the highest accuracy of voice-recognition results. Specifically:

- Only high-quality microphones and tape recording or digital recording devices should be used.
- The subjects should be recorded in a quiet room with low reverberation and no other speakers or background noises.
- The interrogation should contain a sufficient amount of speech. One minute of net speech is required as a minimum. *Net speech* is speech by the subject that is uninter-

Table 3.4
Types of Speaker Recognition Tasks

Type Number	Brief Description
Type 1	*One unknown + multiple suspects (knowns).* This kind of task is similar to closed-set speaker identification.
Type 2	*One unknown + one suspect.* This scenario might arise from a bomb threat traced to a single-occupant residence.
Type 3	*Two unknowns; are they of the same speaker?* This scenario might arise during an investigation in which investigators want to know if the speakers in two separate surveillance tapes are in fact the same speaker.
Type 4	*One unknown + no suspects.* In this scenario, a bomb threat may have been left from a public telephone, presenting a difficult problem.

rupted by other speakers and does not contain long periods of silence.

- Multiple recording sessions for each suspect are necessary to determine the expected variance in the subject's speech.
- All suspects should be recorded in the same manner and with approximately the same duration of net speech.
- The content of speech spoken by the suspects should be of sufficient variety so that all vowel sounds are produced by the suspect.
- To eliminate the preprocessing time required to segment raw input containing conversations where suspects are involved in a dialogue, multitrack recorders that record the suspect on a separate track from the interrogator should be used.

Next, voice-recognition researchers need to be aware of the type of results that law enforcement agents expect. The format of results must be useful to law enforcement agents. Since the results of cross-validation experiments can be confusing, terminology must be agreed upon to prevent misunderstanding of results.

For researchers to compare the accuracy of two or more forensic voice-recognition systems, a new performance metric is necessary. In Chapter 4 of this monograph, the average percent eliminated (APE) metric is used. The APE metric gives an indication of what percentage of the population can be eliminated from consideration—that is, what percentage of the population is pruned from the search space by using a particular voice-recognition system. The metric is calculated as follows:

$$APE = \text{average}\left(1 - \frac{\text{Position of correct match within list of knowns}}{\text{Population size}}\right) \quad (3.17)$$

Since this metric is normalized by population size, it should be valid regardless of the number of suspects.

Finally, it is necessary to have guidelines for creating databases of reference or suspect speakers. The database would be used as a reference in Type 2 cases, in which there is one unknown speaker and one suspect. The database would be also used as the population of suspects in Type 4 cases, in which there are no suspects. The database would be similar to the fingerprint databases currently in use.

The database would store models of speakers in digital form on mass storage devices. The actual voice recordings could be archived in either digital or analog tape forms. However, the voice recordings have to be of the highest quality available as described above, and must be digitized at high sampling rates. Again, multiple sessions per speaker would be necessary. Finally, other information about the speakers, such as sex, age, dialect, and location, would be necessary to help further prune the search space.

A long-term goal is to build a database of a majority of the speakers in the United States, plus foreign visitors. Since the models for each speaker require approximately 16 kilobytes per person, a database for the entire country of adults (2×10^8) might require a minimum of 3,200 gigabytes of storage. As of this writing, there are optical storage systems with 10 times that capacity and access times of several minutes. Thus, the proposed storage is feasible, if not practical. Data collection, it goes without saying, would be challenging both because of the magnitude of the task and because, unlike fingerprints, voices age, and each personal entry in the database would need to be updated every 10 or 20 years.

In times like these, with terrorism having replaced outright warfare in many circumstances, augmenting files of "mug shots" and fingerprints with voice recordings may not be as far-fetched as it would have seemed as recently as 1990.

SUMMARY

In this chapter, a discussion of ideal speaker-recognition systems has been presented and the details of a system based on principles found in ideal systems have been described. Ideal systems are not possible with the knowledge currently available, but systems based on similar techniques can achieve high performance. Techniques for eliminating channel variation have been described. Finally, procedures for how such systems might be used in forensic settings have been suggested.

References
[1] Wang, H. et al., "A Weighted Distance Measure Based on the Fine Structure of Feature Space: Application to Speaker Recognition," *ICASSP,* 1990, pp. 273–276.
[2] Savic, M. and Sorensen, J., "Phoneme Based Speaker Verification," *ICASSP,* 1992, pp. 165–168.

[3] Matsui, Tomoko and Furui, Sadaoki, "Comparison of Text-Independent Speaker Recognition Methods Using VQ-Distortion and Discrete/Continuous HMMs," *ICASSP,* 1992, pp. 157–160.
[4] Linde, Y., Buzo, A., and Gray, R., "An Algorithm for Vector Quantizer Design," *IEEE Transactions on Communications,* Vol. COM-28, No. 1, Jan. 1980, pp. 84–95.
[5] Beyer, William H., *CRC Standard Mathematical Tables,* 28th ed., Boca Raton, FL: CRC Press, Inc., 1987.
[6] Rudasi, Laszlo and Zahorian, Stephen A., "Text-Independent Talker Identification with Neural Networks," *ICASSP,* 1991, pp. 389–392.
[7] Rosenberg, A. E. and Soong, F. K., "Recent Research in Automatic Speaker Recognition," in *Advances in Speech Signal Processing,* New York: Marcel Dekker, Inc., 1992.

Experimental Results 4

In this chapter, the results of experiments performed on the voice-recognition system described in Chapter 3 will be presented. We will describe the results of experiments concerning the length of test utterances, the number of known speakers, the effect of filtering and channel variation, and the ability of the system to perform correctly in mock forensic cases.

In experiments in which the effects of modifying process parameters were examined, the modified parameters will be noted, and the reader may assume that all other process steps are the same as those described in Chapter 3.

TEST UTTERANCE LENGTH EXPERIMENTS

This experiment was used to determine the effects of test utterance length on recognition performance. Forensic voice-recognition systems must be able to perform accurately even with short test utterances, since many forensic exemplars will be of short duration—for example, "There is a bomb in Centennial Park. You have thirty minutes."[1] The population for this experiment consisted of speakers from the TIMIT Database.[2]

---

1. This was the text of the telephone threat delivered at the 1996 Olympic bombing at Centennial Park in Atlanta, Georgia.
2. See Chapter 2 (p. 33) for a discussion of the TIMIT Database.

- Set 1: 22 males from the New England dialect region (DR). (DR1-males);
- Set 2: 25 males from the Northern dialect region. (DR2-males);
- Set 3: 25 females from the New England dialect region. (DR1-females);
- Set 4: 18 females from the Northern dialect region. (DR2-females).

Recognition performance was measured using test utterances of varying length. They were taken from the SA1 and SA2 sentences, which are the same for all speakers in the database. The remaining eight sentences were used for training.

Figure 4.1 shows an overview of the data flow in this experiment. In this figure and all similar figures to follow in this chapter, the standard components of the voice-recognition system are shown as white rectangles. These standard components follow the procedures described in Chapter 3. The shaded rectangle in this figure and subsequent figures shows which part of the standard process has been modified for the experiment. In this case, a subset of the test data is used for creating models of unknown speakers.

The standard feature-extraction procedure was followed for this experiment. The speech waveforms were sampled at 16 kHz, quantized with 14 bits, and windowed at 4-ms intervals with 16-ms Hamming windows. By using energy and zero crossing rate, a voiced/unvoiced decision was made for each window. The nonvoiced windows were discarded. Then, for each window, the lowest three formant frequencies were determined using LPC, and the inverse spectral coefficients were calculated with an FFT. This process was described in detail in Chapter 3 and was used for the remaining experiments in this chapter.

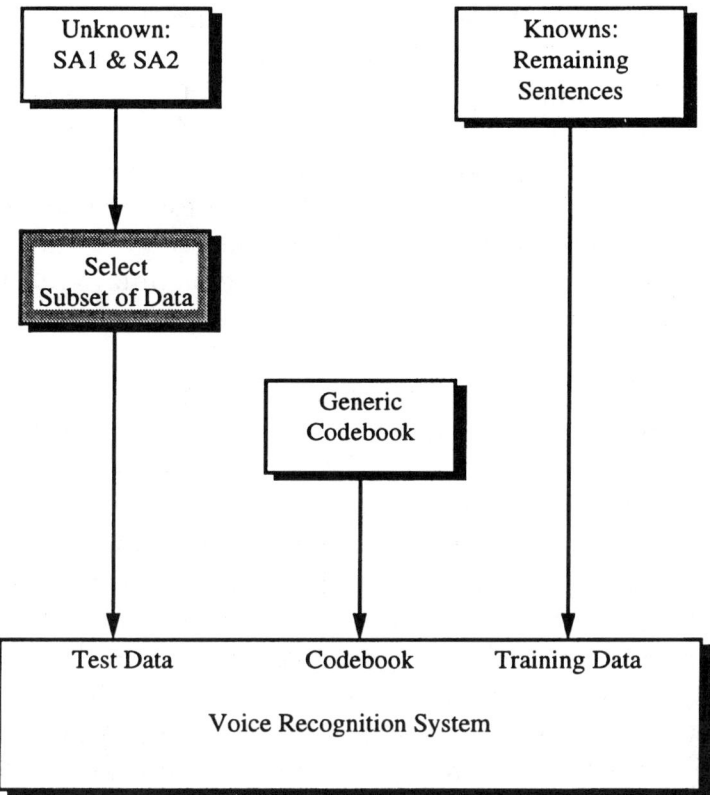

Figure 4.1 Data flow for the test utterance length experiment.

For each of the speakers in the populations sets, a "known" model was created using the features vectors from the eight non-SA sentences. Feature extraction was performed on these waveforms, and the generic codebook was used for segregating vectors into categories. Recall that segregation is based on the lowest three format frequencies. The generic codebook is trained from data taken randomly from the population and was used in most of the experiments in this chapter.

After performing feature extraction on the SA sentences for all the speakers in the population, it was determined that each speaker had at least 400 usable feature vectors. For each speaker, speaker recognition was performed several times with different-sized subsets of the first 400 feature vectors for each speaker.

During the experiments, a subset of test feature vectors was used to create an "unknown" model for the speaker. This model was compared with all the "known" models in the population set. Since the population sets contain speakers of the same sex and dialect, a high degree of similarity exists among them.

Identification was performed by choosing the known speaker with the lowest distortion score, where the distortion score is the weighted sum of the distance between feature vectors in each category from the "known" and "unknown" models. The accuracy of the voice-identification system can be determined since the best match should be the corresponding known speaker. If the best match was not the correct speaker, it was considered to be an error.

This process was repeated for all speakers in the population set; therefore, n^2 comparisons were performed for each population set, where n is the number of speakers in the set. We will use this process, called "the n^2 test" and illustrated in Figure 4.2, throughout the remaining experiments in this chapter.

Error rates were determined by dividing the number of errors by the size of the population set, n.

$$\text{Error Rate} = \frac{\text{Number of Errors}}{n} \qquad (4.1)$$

The results for all four population sets are shown in Figure 4.3.

Performance of the system stabilizes when the number of test frames is greater than 50, which is approximately one-

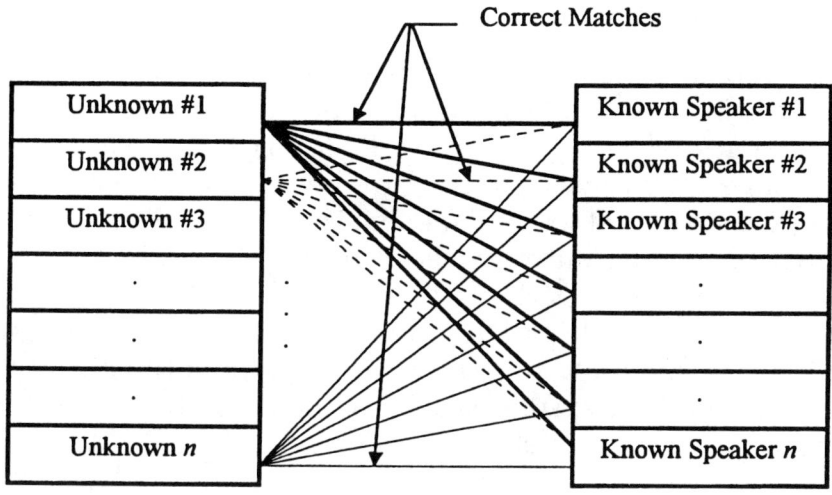

Figure 4.2 The n^2 test.

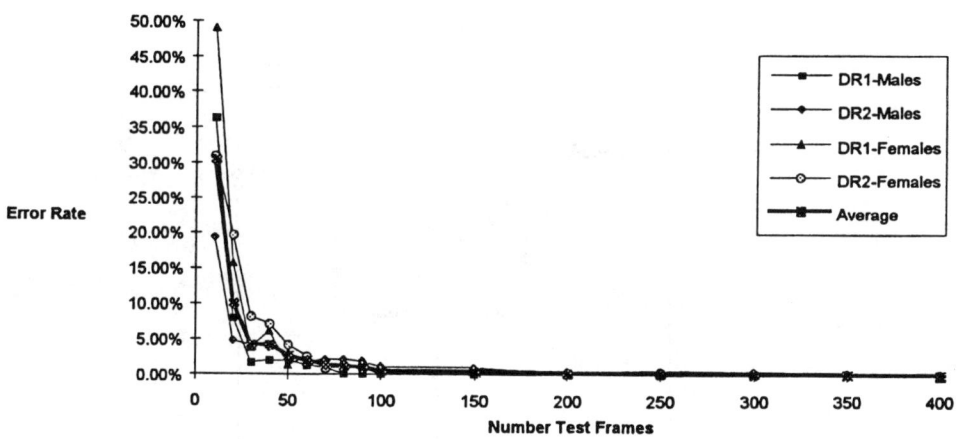

Figure 4.3 Identification error rates versus test utterance length.

fourth of one sentence. Since most voice crimes, such as bomb threats, will be longer than this duration, accurate forensic recognition will be possible.

LARGE POPULATION RESULTS

The purpose of this experiment is to determine the performance of the system with a large population. All speakers from each dialect region of the TIMIT Database were used. The experiment was similar to the previous experiment except that the test exemplars consisted of the SA1 and SA2 sentences in their entirety (see Figure 4.4).

An n^2 test was performed on each dialect region and on the male and female populations. The APE metric was used in this experiment to determine how the performance of the voice-recognition system scaled with population size. (See Chapter 3 for a complete discussion of APE.)

$$APE = \text{average}\left(1 - \frac{\text{Position of correct match within list of knowns}}{\text{Population size}}\right)$$

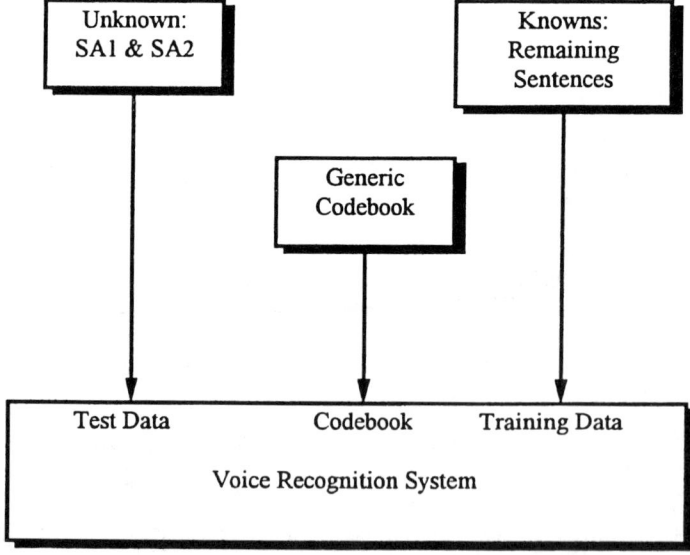

Figure 4.4 Data flow for large population experiment.

In Table 4.1, the results of recognition experiments for each dialect region of the TIMIT Database are shown. The APE scores for dialect regions with smaller populations are worse simply because of the granularity of the APE calculation.

The results of experiments using all the males and all the females are shown in Table 4.2.

These results indicate that as the size of the population increases, the percentage of individuals that can be eliminated stays fairly constant and may even improve. This fact is a strong indicator that successful voice recognition can be performed on large populations, such as the population of an entire city, state, or country.

Table 4.1
APE Result by Dialect Region

Dialect Region	Number of Speakers	APE Score
1	37	0.972973
2	65	0.984615
3	66	0.984618
4	65	0.983905
5	65	0.984375
6	32	0.968750
7	66	0.984615
8	24	0.958333

Table 4.2
APE Results for All Males and Females

Set	Number of Speakers	APE Score
Males	290	0.996
Females	130	0.992

FILTERED DATA TEST

The purpose of this test was to determine the effects of filtering the input data to the system. In this experiment, both the data for the knowns and unknowns were low-pass filtered with a 3,500 Hz cutoff filter (see Figure 4.5). This filter is roughly equivalent to typical telephone-line filter characteristics.

Table 4.3 reports the results of the n^2 tests of the male population in each dialect region using the normal VQ codebook and leaving the other test conditions unchanged.

The test was repeated with a VQ codebook trained with filtered data. Specifically, a new generic codebook would be

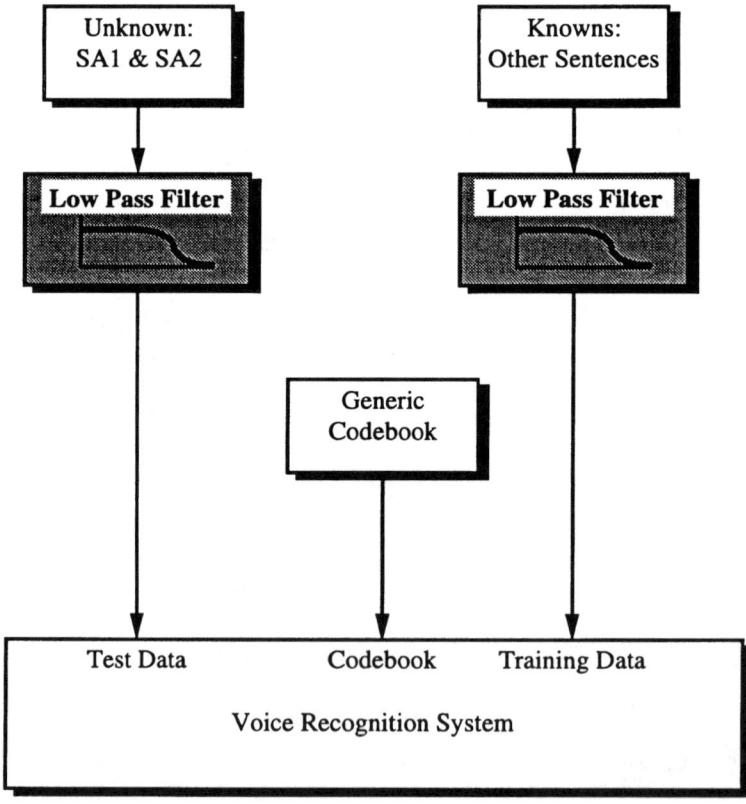

Figure 4.5 Data flow for filtered data experiment.

Table 4.3
Preliminary Filtered Data
Test Results

Dialect Region	Number of Errors (Males)
1	11
2	17
3	27
4	19
5	21
6	8
7	24
8	8
Total	136

trained to model the clusters in filtered speech. Again, the input data was taken from a group of randomly selected speakers as illustrated in Figure 4.6. The results are shown in Table 4.4.

In the next experiment, filtering was simulated by using only the lower harmonics of the frequency spectrum during the category comparison step of the voice-recognition process. This reduces the amount of processing time significantly compared to the digital filtering computations of the previous experiment. This is illustrated in Figure 4.7, and the results are shown in Table 4.5.

Unfortunately, this technique does not actually simulate filtering, since none of the points below the 60th harmonic are affected. This technique is valid, however, for demonstrating that segments of the spectrum that have been corrupted by random additive noise can be removed from the comparison process simply by removing the parts of the spectrum that are affected by the noise. The cost of this removal of spectral points, in terms of recognition performance, is proportional to the number of points removed from the spectrum.

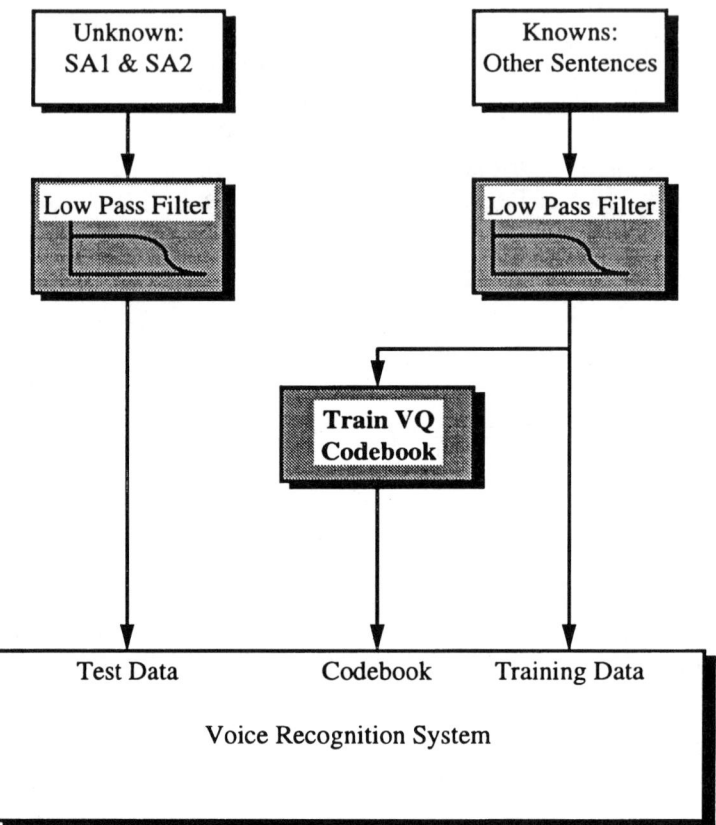

Figure 4.6 Data flow for filtered codebook data experiment.

As a comparison, the experiment using all harmonics was performed, as illustrated in Figure 4.8, with results shown in Table 4.6. As expected, recognition using all the harmonics and no filtering is very accurate.

CHANNEL COMPENSATION TESTS

In most forensic voice-recognition scenarios, voice exemplars will be recorded through some unknown channel. A major part of the degradation of the signal will be caused by filtering.

Table 4.4
Filter Data With Filtered
Data VQ Codebook

Dialect Region	Number of Errors (Males)
1	10
2	22
3	19
4	20
5	17
6	11
7	22
8	11
Total	132

The previous experiments show how filtering of the exemplars degrades recognition performance. Since the filter used on the unknown is not precisely known in real forensic settings, we need to devise a method for determining what the unknown filter is in addition to whom the unknown speaker is.

To perform controllable experiments dealing with the effects of filtering, the TIMIT Database was used so that the data could be corrupted in controllable ways. The basic idea is to corrupt the unknown exemplar with some kind of filter and then devise methods for filtering the knowns to match the filtering of the unknown.

Average Filter Compensation Technique Experiment

In the first experiment, the unknown speech sample comprised the TIMIT SA1 and SA1 sentences. The training data consisted of the remaining eight sentences. An experiment was performed to determine the effects of filter mismatch and

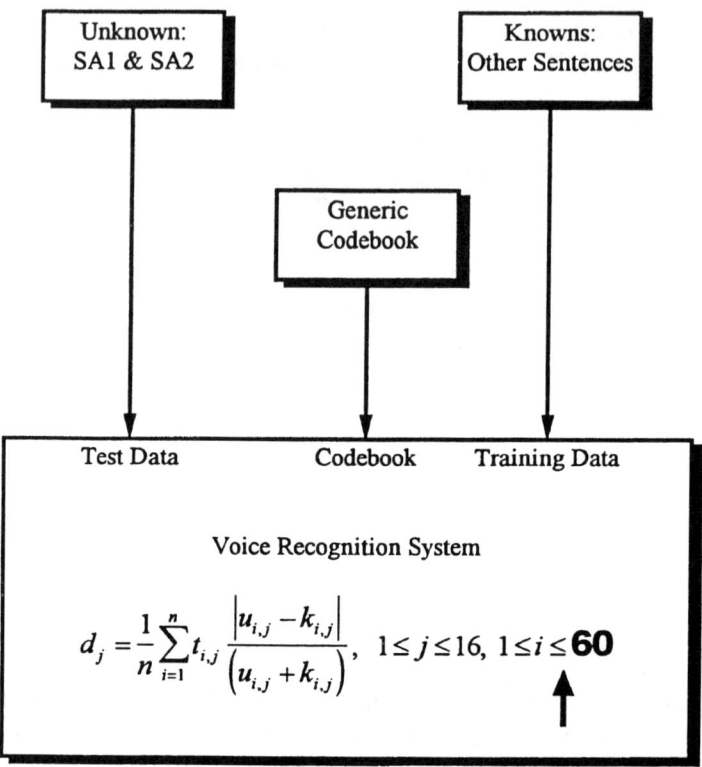

Figure 4.7 Data flow for unfiltered data, 1-60 harmonics experiment.

the ability of the average filter compensation technique to correct the problem. The filter used was a 13th-order Butterworth filter with a cutoff at 4000 Hz. Both male and female speakers from TIMIT DR1 (37 speakers) were used. The APE scores were determined for various situations, as indicated in Table 4.7. Figure 4.9 illustrates the procedure.

The experiments were performed for different subsections of the spectrum. The results are consolidated in Tables 4.8 and 4.9 below.

The results show that without channel mismatch the recognition accuracy is very high and that the average filter compensation does not cause significant loss in accuracy when

Table 4.5
Unfiltered Data, 1-60
Harmonics

Dialect Region	Number of Errors (Males)
1	0
2	6
3	5
4	1
5	3
6	1
7	1
8	0
Total	17

no channel mismatch exists. The results also show how poor performance is when channel mismatch does occur and that average filter compensation can improve accuracy, especially at the lower harmonics.

Finally, the results show that if the unknown is filtered and the knowns are filtered using the same filter, then fairly high accuracy can still be achieved. This result led to the implementation of the rehumanizing filter technique.

Rehumanizing Filter Technique Experiment

In the next experiment, the rehumanizing filter technique described in Chapter 3 was evaluated. Again, the unknown speech sample was composed of the TIMIT SA1 and SA1 sentences filtered with a 13th-order Butterworth filter with a cutoff of 4,000 Hz. The knowns were filtered with several different filters created by varying the order and cutoff parameters. The goal was to determine if the proper filter parameters could be determined by examining properties of the recognition scores at different parameter configurations. This is illustrated in Figure 4.10.

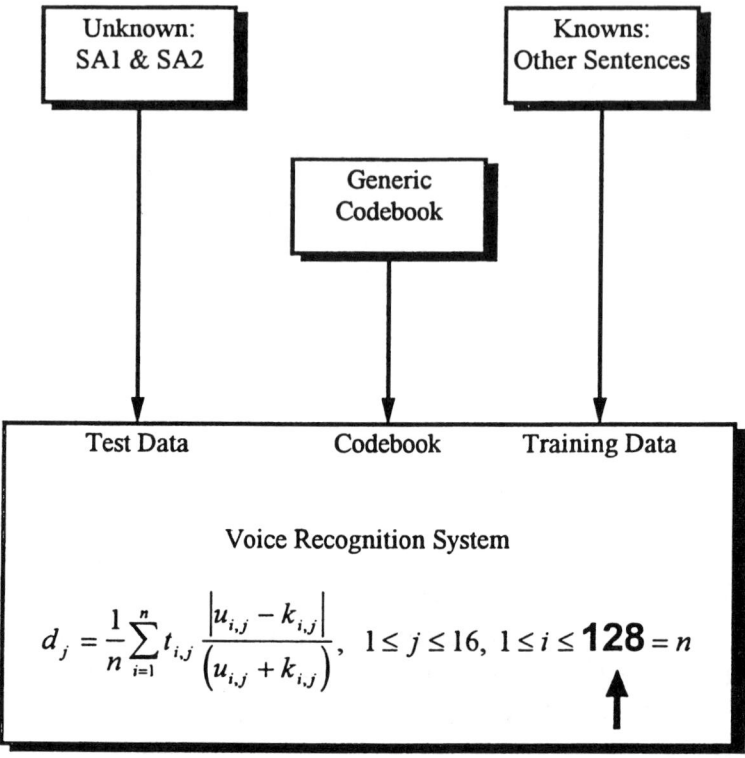

Figure 4.8 Data flow for unfiltered data, 1-128 harmonics experiment.

The population sets for these experiments were the TIMIT DR1 male set with 22 speakers and the DR1 female set with 15 speakers. An n^2 test was performed on each group separately. The distortion scores for each comparison at a specific filter value were analyzed to create the graphs shown in Figures 4.11–4.14.

These graphs show that standard deviation, the minimum, and average of the raw scores all are *minimized* when the order of the filter used for filtering the knowns correctly matches the order of the filter used for filtering the unknown. Thus, by having three independent measures of filter-order correctness, the choice of the correcting filter for the known

Table 4.6
UnfilteredData, 1-128
Harmonics

Dialect Region	Number of Errors (Males)
1	1
2	2
3	1
4	2
5	0
6	0
7	1
8	0
Total	7

will be more accurate. The graphs also show that the recognition performance, measured in terms of the average percent of the population eliminated (APE), is maximized when the filter match is correct. The peak in the APE graphs gives an estimate of the best possible recognition performance that can be expected by guessing the unknown filter, since at the peak, the filter used for the knowns and unknowns is the same. This value is less than what is achievable under the ideal conditions of no filtering for either knowns or unknowns. The complete set of graphs is available from the authors.

SECONDARY PARAMETERS

The purpose of these tests is to investigate the effectiveness of secondary parameters for clarifying comparisons where the original methods are not definitive. The values of several secondary parameters were calculated for both the training and test utterances in the TIMIT Database. *Pitch* is the average pitch of the input data. *Moment*$_{JP}$, which is equivalent to Koster's jaw position parameter [1], is calculated as follows:

Table 4.7
Average Filter Compensation Technique Experimental Conditions

Kind of Data	Description
Clean unknown, clean known	In this experiment, both the known and unknowns were clean recordings (unfiltered). This is the best possible situation
Clean unknown, clean known, normalized	In this experiment both the known and unknowns were clean recordings (unfiltered); however, the average filter compensation technique was applied. This experiment would determine whether normalization caused performance degradation when the channels *were* the same
Filtered unknowns, clean knowns	In this experiment, the unknown was filtered and the knowns were not filtered. This is the worse possible situation since the channels do not match and no compensation is performed.
Filtered unknowns, filtered knowns	In this experiment, both the known and unknowns were filtered. This experiment will determine how the loss of high-frequency information affects performance when the channels are matched.
Filtered unknowns, clean knowns, normalized	In this experiment, the unknown was filtered and the knowns were not filtered. The average filter compensation technique was applied. This experiment will determine if the average filter compensation technique can correct channel-mismatch problems.
Filtered unknowns, filtered knowns, normalized	In this experiment, both the known and unknowns were filtered, and the average filter compensation technique was applied. Again, does normalization degrade performance when the channels are matched?

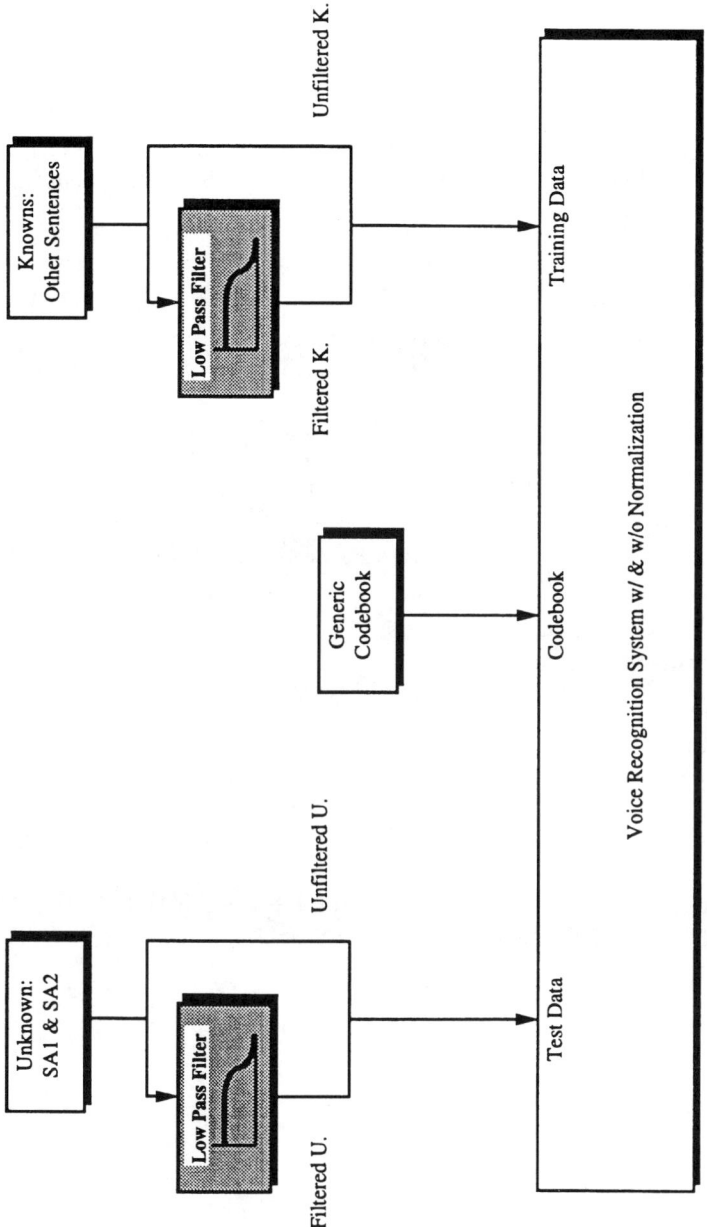

Figure 4.9 Data flow for filter effects experiment.

Table 4.8
Filter Effects

	Average Percent Eliminated (U = Unknowns, K = Knowns)			
Harmonics	Clean U Clean K	Clean U Clean K Normalized	Filter U Clean K	Filter U Clean K Normalized
1-128	.973	.968	.510	.724
1-60	.973	.961	.510	.775
1-30	.970	.949	.697	.744
31-60	.946	.946	.756	.756
61-90	.918	.918	.550	.550

Table 4.9
More Filter Effects

	Average Percent Eliminated	
Harmonics	Filter U Filter K	Filter U Filter K Normalized
1-128	.965	.928
1-60	.965	.932

$$\text{Moment}_{JP} = m_2 - m_1^2 \qquad (4.2)$$

The first and second moments of the FFT spectrum, m_1 and m_2, are defined as follows:

$$m_0 = \sum_{n=0}^{N-1} F_n$$

$$m_1 = \frac{1}{m_0} \sum_{n=0}^{N-1} F_n n \qquad (4.3)$$

$$m_2 = \frac{1}{m_0} \sum_{n=0}^{N-1} F_n n^2$$

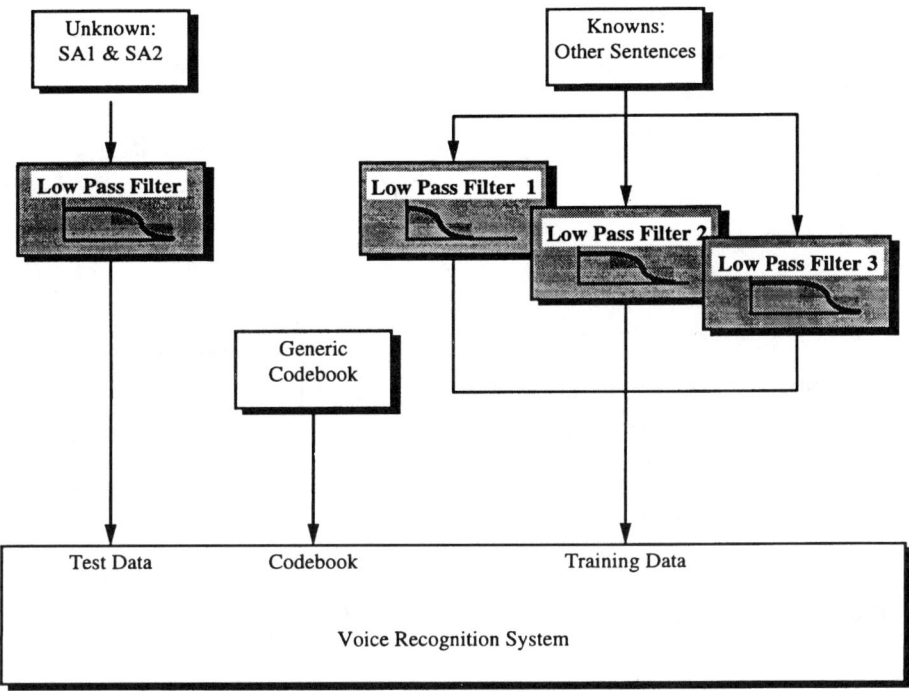

Figure 4.10 Data flow for rehumanizing filter experiment.

where m_i is the *ith* moment function, F_n is the energy at the *nth* harmonic of the spectrum, and N is the number of points in the spectrum (128).

The average of *Moment*$_{\text{JP}}$ and the standard deviations above and below the average of *Moment*$_{\text{JP}}$ were calculated (moment average, high STD, low STD). These calculations are shown below:

$$\text{Moment Average} = \frac{1}{n}\sum_{i=1}^{n} \text{Moment}_{\text{JP},i} \qquad (4.4)$$

where *Moment*$_{\text{JP},i}$ is the *ith* value in the set of *Moment*$_{\text{JP}}$ values.

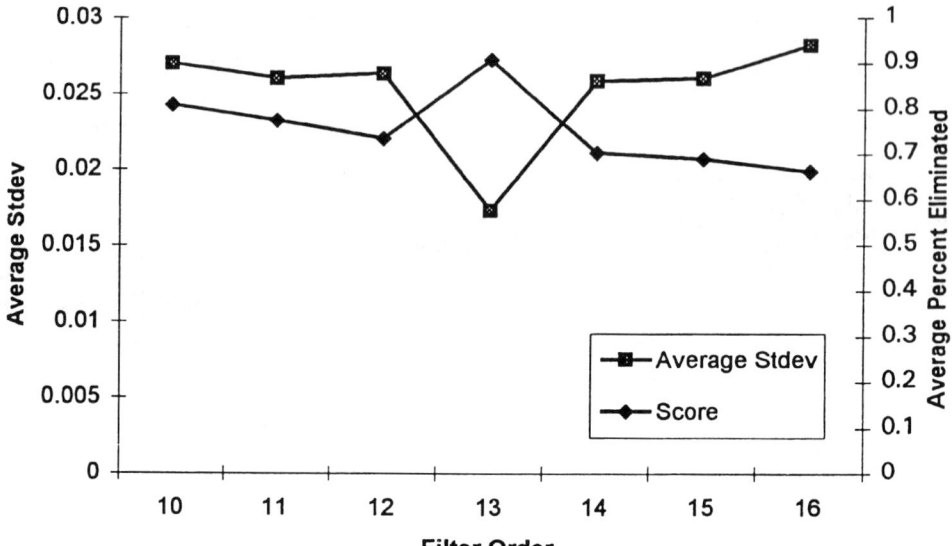

Figure 4.11 Average standard deviation (DR1 females).

$$\text{Low STD} = \left(\frac{1}{(l-1)} \sum_{i=1}^{l} (Moment_{\text{JPL},i} - \text{Moment Average})\right)^{1/2}$$

(4.5)

where l is the number of $Moment_{\text{JP}}$ values that are less than moment average and $Moment_{\text{JPL},i}$ are those values.

$$\text{High STD} = \left(\frac{1}{(h-1)} \sum_{i=1}^{h} (Moment_{\text{JPH},i} - \text{Moment Average})\right)^{1/2}$$

(4.6)

where h is the number of $Moment_{\text{JP}}$ values that are greater than moment average and $Moment_{\text{JPH},i}$ are those values.

Since the range of jaw position values is determined by the physical dimensions of the speakers' vocal tracts, it was hypothesized to contain useful information for voice recognition.

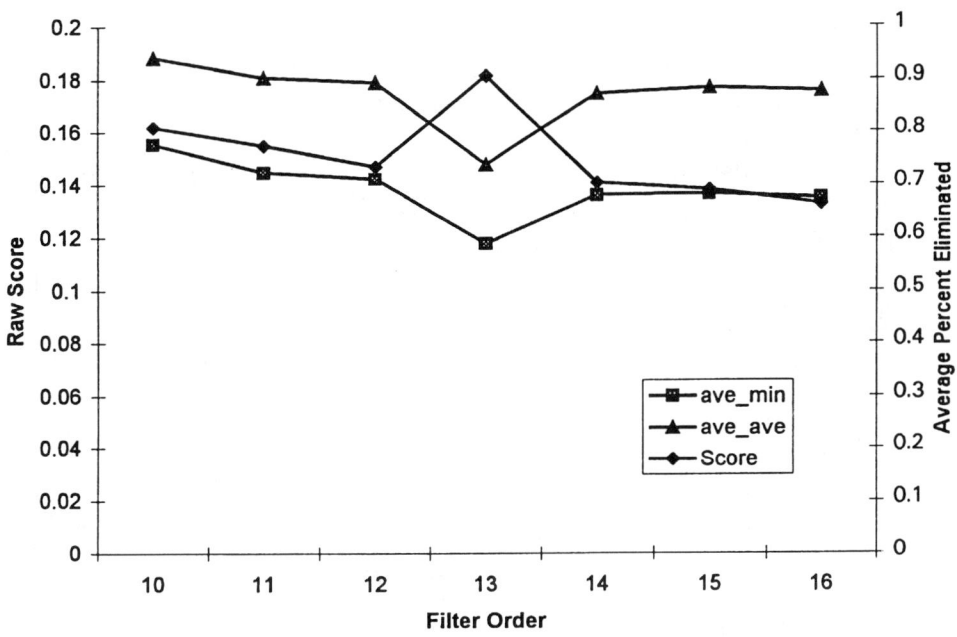

Figure 4.12 Average minimum and average (DR1 females).

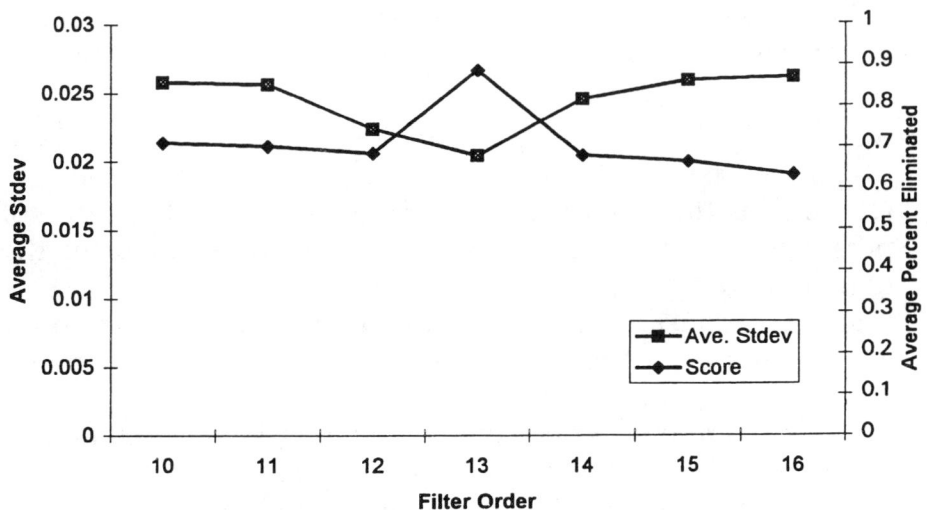

Figure 4.13 Average standard deviation (DR1 males).

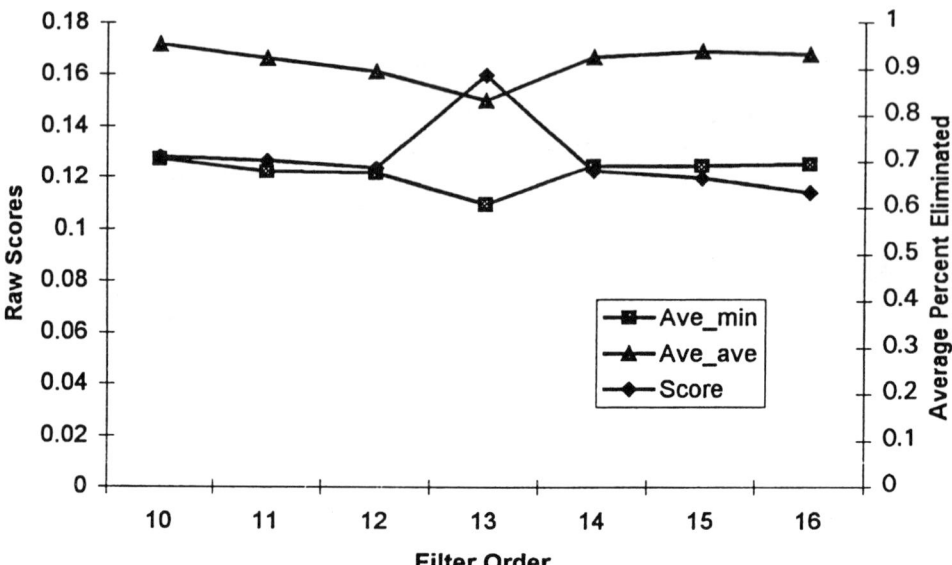

Figure 4.14 Average minimum and average (DR1 males).

For each secondary parameter considered, the distortion value between the known and unknown exemplars was used for recognition. The distortion was calculated as follows:

$$d_p = |u_p - k_p| \qquad (4.7)$$

where d_p is the distortion for parameter p, u_p is the value of parameter p for the unknown, k_p is the value of p for the known, and p is either pitch, moment average, low STD, or high STD. Consequently, the known with least distortion for a parameter was chosen as the best match for that parameter. This is illustrated in Figure 4.15.

The combined effect of the secondary parameters was determined by calculating the distortion for the product of the four parameters after they had been normalized. This calculation is performed as shown below:

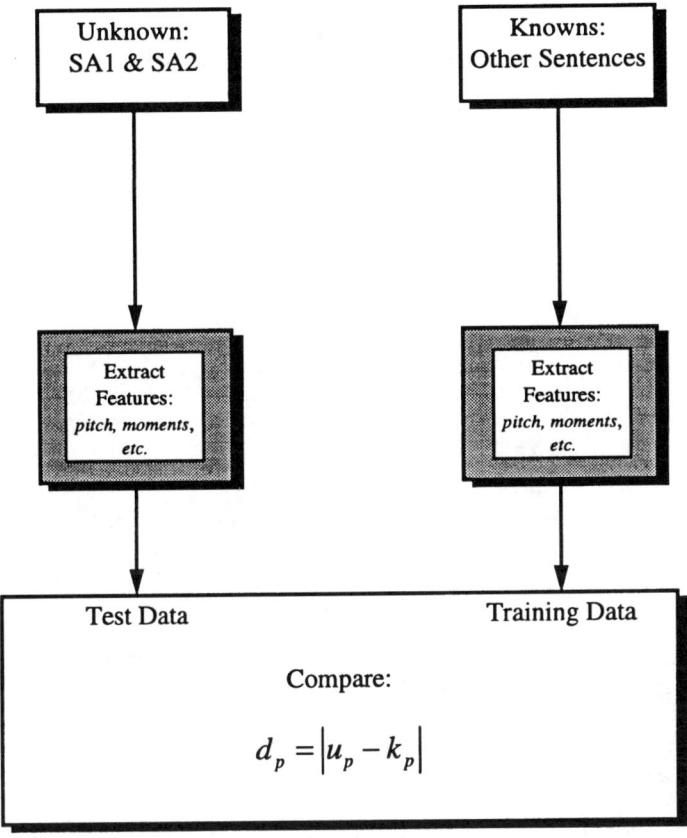

Figure 4.15 Data flow for secondary parameters experiment.

$$d_{prod} = 1 - \prod_{\text{All } p} (1 - normal(d_p)) \qquad (4.8)$$

where d_{prod} is the combined distortion, $normal(d_p)$ is the position of d_p on normal distribution curve, and p is either pitch, moment average, low STD, or high STD. An n^2 test was performed for each of the TIMIT dialect regions. The average positions of d_p and d_{prod} for the correct match among all of the scores for is shown in Table 4.10.

Table 4.10
Secondary Parameter Effectiveness

Dialect Region	Pitch	Moment Average	Average Position Low STD	Average Position High STD	Product
1	3.90	5.97	13.54	5.86	2.29
2	6.20	11.60	21.86	13.00	4.66
3	7.67	10.35	25.38	12.06	4.41
4	5.57	11.30	22.14	10.46	3.35
5	6.22	10.50	24.78	9.70	3.98
6	2.53	7.53	10.65	7.00	2.6
7	5.35	12.09	23.07	11.16	5.03
8	2.30	3.67	9.17	3.29	1.87
Average	4.96	9.12	18.82	9.06	3.52

The results show that *pitch* is the most effective of the secondary parameters and that the product of the four parameter yields the best results.

Secondary Parameter Usage

The purpose of these experiments was to test the effectiveness of each of the secondary parameters for clarifying decisions that were deemed inconclusive by the original algorithm.

When the comparison of speakers is performed two at a time, the effectiveness of the comparison is determined as follows:

$$r = \frac{|d_1 - d_2|}{d_1 + d_2} \quad (4.9)$$

where d_1 and d_2 are the distortion scores for the two speakers and r is a measure of how far apart the two scores are.

A threshold for approximately how large r should be to ensure a correct decision with a high degree of confidence is determined by:

$$\text{thresh} = \frac{\text{cutoff}}{\sqrt{(\text{number of vectors}) \cdot (\text{number of points in spectrum})}}$$
(4.10)

where *cutoff* is a user-definable parameter that was determined by trial and error, and the value within the square root is an indication of how much information is available for making the comparison. If more information is available, then the difference between d_1 and d_2 does not need to be as large to guarantee a correct decision with a specified confidence level.

If $r < thresh$, then the comparison is deemed to be inconclusive. If a comparison is deemed to be inconclusive, then the secondary parameters are used for determining the decision. The *cutoff* parameter can be increased to require that the system have greater separation between speakers for a decision to be deemed conclusive. The logic in this procedure is illustrated in a flow diagram in Figure 4.16.

The abbreviations in Table 4.11 are used to describe the results of the next experiment.

Tables 4.12–4.15 show the performance of each of the four secondary parameters used individually during n^2 tests on the TIMIT Database. To force a large number of inconclusive comparisons, only the lower 60 points in the spectrum were used for these experiments. This was necessary to guarantee a sufficient number of instances in which secondary parameters might come into play.

Tables 4.12–4.15 show that the secondary parameters are somewhat effective for clarifying recognition decisions where the coarse/fine segregation algorithm is inconclusive. Thus, the secondary parameters are somewhat orthogonal to the distortion scores provided by the original algorithm.

Effects of Varying the Cutoff Value

The purpose of these experiments is to determine the effects of varying the value of *cutoff*.

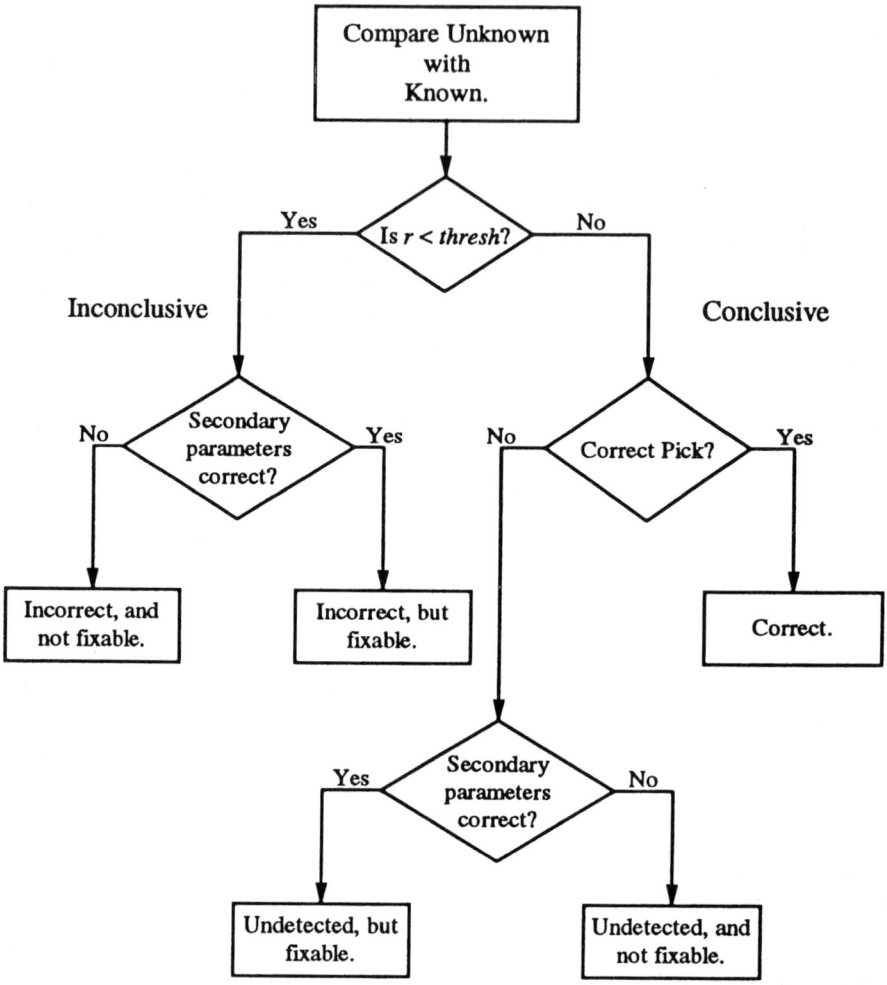

Figure 4.16 Execution flow for secondary parameter usage experiment.

Tables 4.16 and 4.17 show that raising the cutoff value does not improve the resulting recognition.

Best-Case Secondary Parameter Usage

The purpose of this experiment was to determine the best possible performance of the voice-recognition system when

Table 4.11
Decision Names

Abbreviation	Description
Inc Fix	The number of inconclusive comparisons that were correctly resolved by secondary parameters.
Inc Wrong	The number of inconclusive comparisons that were incorrectly resolved by secondary parameters.
Undet Fix	The number of undetected misclassifications that could have been resolved by the secondary parameters.
Undet Wrong	The number of undetected misclassifications that the secondary parameters would not have resolved.
Total	The total number of errors = Inc Wrong + Undet Fix + Undet Wrong

Table 4.12
Pitch, *Cutoff* = 3.0, 1-60 Harmonics, Total = 27

Dialect Region	Inc Fix	Inc Wrong	Undet Fix	Undet Wrong
1	1	0	0	0
2	11	7	3	4
3	11	2	4	1
4	8	1	0	0
5	5	2	0	0
6	2	0	0	0
7	5	3	0	0
8	0	0	0	0
Totals	43	15	7	5

Table 4.13
Moment Average, $Cutoff = 3.0$, 1-60 Harmonics, Total = 28

Dialect Region	Inc Fix	Inc Wrong	Undet Fix	Undet Wrong
1	1	0	0	0
2	12	6	3	4
3	11	2	4	1
4	7	2	0	0
5	5	2	0	0
6	2	0	0	0
7	4	4	0	0
8	0	0	0	0
Totals	42	16	7	5

Table 4.14
Low STD, $Cutoff = 3.0$, 1-60 Harmonics, Total = 43

Dialect Region	Inc Fix	Inc Wrong	Undet Fix	Undet Wrong
1	1	0	0	0
2	7	11	6	1
3	3	10	1	4
4	5	4	0	0
5	4	3	0	0
6	0	2	0	0
7	7	1	0	0
8	0	0	0	0
Totals	27	31	7	5

secondary parameters are used to resolve inconclusive comparisons. In this experiment, the full 128-point spectrum was used as opposed to the lower 60 points used in the previously reported experiments. The results are shown in Table 4.18.

This experiment shows that secondary parameters can help improve recognition performance slightly but that the original algorithm has better performance on average.

Table 4.15
High STD, *Cutoff* = 3.0, 1-60 Harmonics, Total = 25

Dialect Region	Inc Fix	Inc Wrong	Undet Fix	Undet Wrong
1	1	0	0	0
2	11	7	4	3
3	12	1	5	0
4	9	0	0	0
5	6	1	0	0
6	2	0	0	0
7	4	4	0	0
8	0	0	0	0
Totals	45	13	9	3

Table 4.16
Combined, *Cutoff* = 4.0 1-60 Harmonics, Total = 23

Dialect Region	Inc Fix	Inc Wrong	Undet Fix	Undet Wrong
1	1	0	0	0
2	13	7	3	2
3	16	3	4	0
4	13	1	3	0
5	7	2	0	0
6	3	0	0	0
7	0	2	0	0
8	8	0	0	0
Totals	61	15	10	2

MOCK FORENSIC CASES

To examine how the system would perform in a forensic setting, the system was tested with mock forensic data. An agent of the NCSBI supplied us with tape recordings of several mock forensic cases. The recordings were made using standard law enforcement equipment and procedures.

Table 4.17
Combined, *Cutoff* = 9.0 1-60 Harmonics, Total = 78

Dialect Region	Inc Fix	Inc Wrong	Undet Fix	Undet Wrong
1	10	0	0	0
2	47	25	0	0
3	72	18	0	0
4	63	13	0	0
5	37	7	0	0
6	8	4	0	0
7	51	10	0	0
8	1	1	0	0
Totals	289	78	0	0

Table 4.18
Combined, *Cutoff* = 4.0, 1-128 Harmonics, Total = 5 of 420 Speakers (98.8% Accuracy)

Dialect Region	Inc Fix	Inc Wrong	Undet Fix	Undet Wrong
1	0	0	0	0
2	4	0	0	0
3	1	2	2	1
4	1	0	0	0
5	0	0	0	0
6	0	0	0	0
7	2	0	0	0
8	0	0	0	0
Totals	8	2	2	1

SBI Case 1

This case was based on an actual homicide. The victim received a threat on an answering machine. By tracing the call, the authorities were able to come up with six female suspects. The task was to identify which of the six known female speakers matched the unknown speaker who had left the threatening message. This is an example of Type 1 voice recognition (see Chapter 3).

The major difficulties in this case were that the unknown recording was short and noisy and that the training data for the known speakers consisted of only one session per speaker. There was also an uneven amount of data per speaker.

The basic strategy was first to determine what part of the frequency spectrum worked best for this specific case. Then, *cross-validation*, a technique for testing the inherent accuracy of classifiers (recognizers), was used to determine a reliability measurement for our decision. Cross-validation consists of performing repetitive tests of different portions of available input data to simulate the performance of the recognizer on larger sets of data. The details of this technique will be described later.

A test was performed to determine which part of the spectrum contained the most information. First, each of the files for the known speakers was broken into two segments: a segment called the *pseudounknown* that was of approximately the same duration as the real unknown and the remainder of the file, called the *pseudoknown*. This is illustrated in Figure 4.17.

By performing n^2 tests on the pseudounknowns versus the pseudoknowns, an estimate of the system's performance could be made since the correct answer for these comparisons was known in advance. The system was able to match correctly each pseudounknown with its corresponding pseudoknown in each of these pseudotests.

The same pseudotests with different segments of the frequency spectrum revealed the relative merits of each spectral band. The graph in Figure 4.18 shows the number of identification errors when only certain segments of the frequency spectrum were used.

As a result, for Case 1, only the lowest 60 harmonics were used in the experiments that followed, since those harmonics

138 *Voice Recognition*

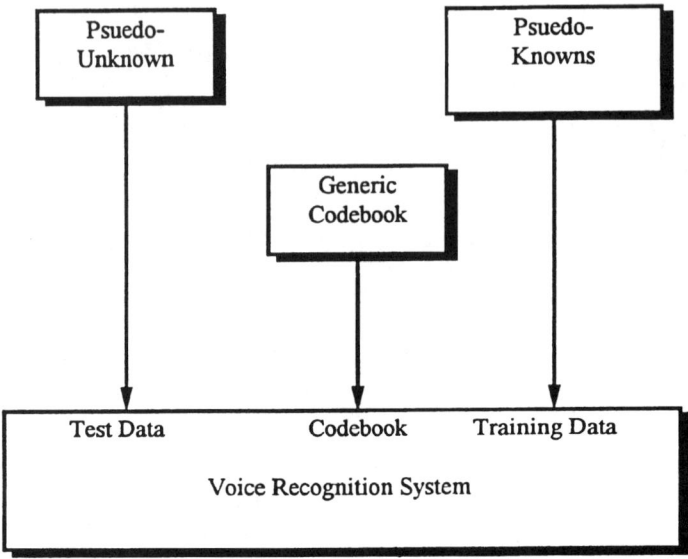

Figure 4.17 Pseudotest data flow.

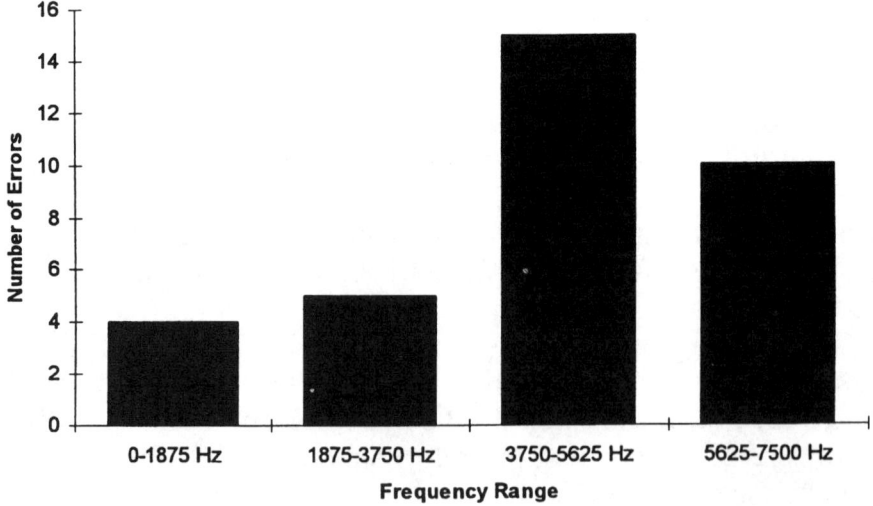

Figure 4.18 Frequency test.

corresponded to the 0–3,750 Hz frequency range, where the voice-recognition system had the best performance. The higher harmonics were most likely corrupted by noise in the recording channel.

The strategy for performing cross-validation was to perform multiple identification experiments on different sections of the data. For example, the first experiment might use only the first 10 seconds of the recordings for each known speaker. In the second experiment, only speech in the 10–20-second interval of known recordings would be used. Similarly, the third experiment might use only the 20–30-second interval. (See Figure 4.19.)

For each experiment, a model is created for a section of the recording for each known suspect. The model for the unknown is compared with these models. This process is repeated for each experiment where different sections of the suspect's recording are used to create the suspect's model. A total score for each known suspect is determined by averaging together the distortions for that suspect from each of the experiments. Since the amount of speech data was limited, cross-validation provided a method for extracting the most information from the small amount of input data available. The amount of training data per known speaker was normalized to prevent bias.

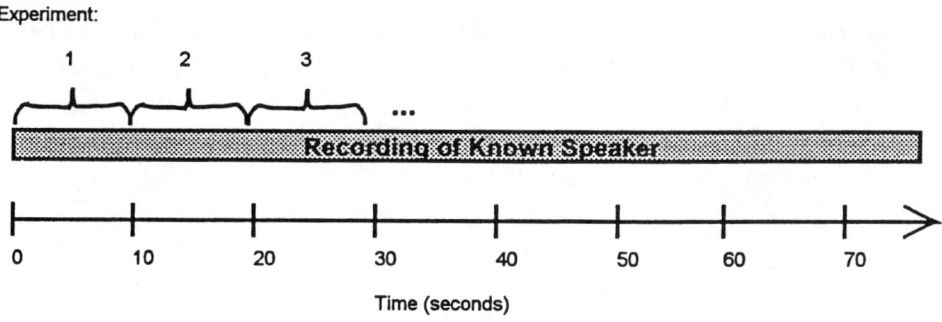

Figure 4.19 Cross-validation.

Three types of cross-validation were examined. In the first type, the sections of data for each experiment were allowed to overlap each other. (See Figure 4.20.) Thus, more training data is available for each experiment; however, each experiment is correlated to the others.

Conversely, if no overlap is used, the experiments will be more independent, but with less training data available for each experiment. (See Figure 4.21.)

The third type of cross-validation consists of eliminating *short-file outliers* from consideration. A short-file outlier is a suspect who has a very poor recognition score using either of the first two cross-validation techniques and has the shortest data file in the population. If the outlier has a very low probability of having committed the crime, it may be removed from the population. This allows the experiments to be repeated with more input data; that is, the length-normalized files will be longer, since the shortest file was eliminated. (See Figure 4.22.)

The results of the Case 1 analysis are shown in Tables 4.19, 4.20, and 4.21. The boldface rows indicate the speaker in the population with the best (lowest) average raw score for the experiments within each cross-validation procedure. The confidence in the best choice was determined by calculating the F-test value between the best choice (the boldfaced entry) and the other choices in the population. The value indicates the confidence in the decision that the average value for the best choice is actually lower than the average for the other speaker in question. Thus, the confidence value of 0.995 for Known A in Table 4.19 means that Speaker F is a better choice than Speaker A, with 99.5% confidence.

Table 4.19 shows the results of cross-validation with five nonoverlapped segments of data and all six suspects in the population. Table 4.20 shows the results of similar experiments but with the short-file outlier (Speaker A) removed. Table 4.21 shows the results of experiments in which an impostor, Impostor #1a, was added to the population.

Experimental Results 141

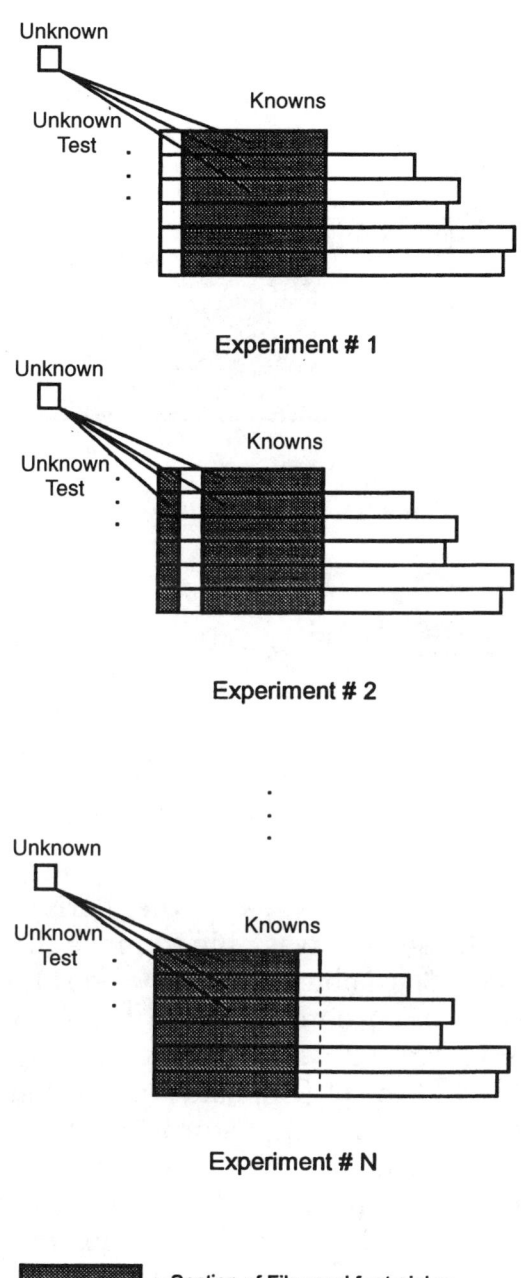

Figure 4.20 Overlapping.

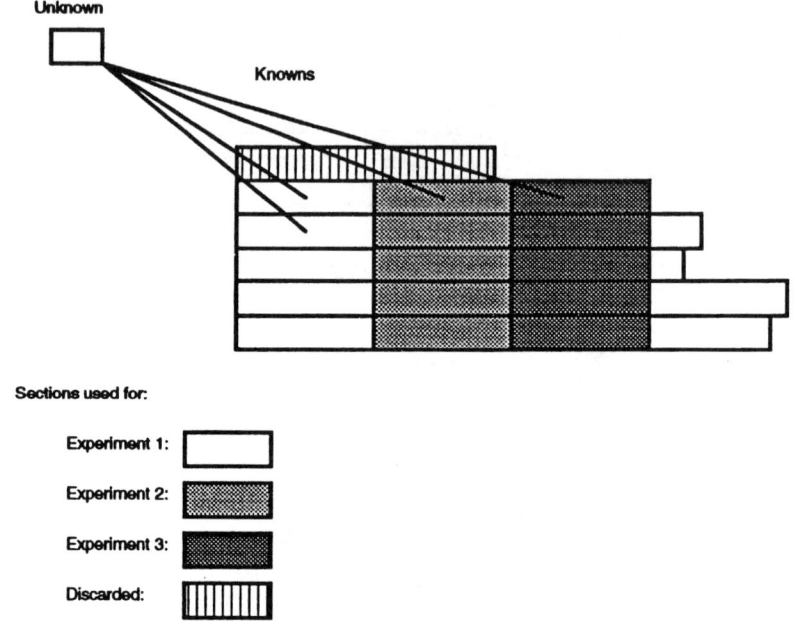

Figure 4.21 Nonoverlapping, length normalized.

According to the SBI agent, the correct choice was Speaker F [2]. The system was able to make this choice with 95% confidence. (See Table 4.20.) However, the system was unable to assign much confidence to the decision that the unknown was in fact one of the six suspects, since adding another speaker to the set (Impostor #1a) caused a different choice for the best match (Impostor #1a). (See Table 4.21.)

Considering the difficulties involved in analyzing this case, we were greatly encouraged by the performance of the system. Furthermore, if the procedures for recording exemplars, as described in Chapter 3, are followed in future forensic cases, the system will be able to put an even higher degree of confidence in its decision.

Experimental Results 143

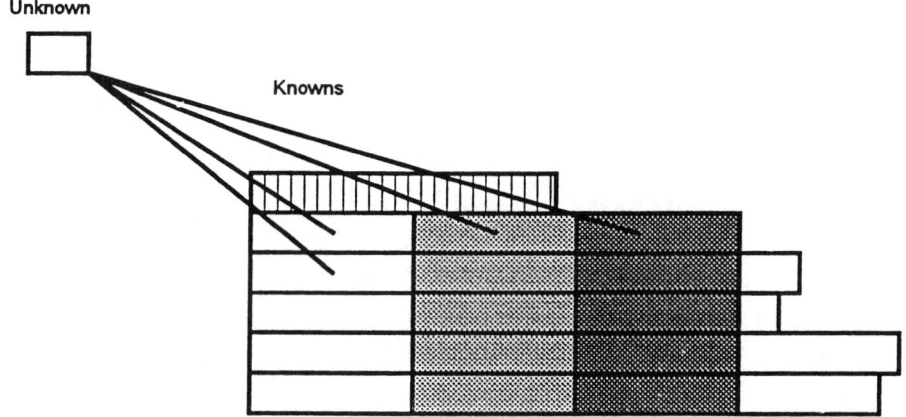

Figure 4.22 Nonoverlapping with speaker 0 discarded.

Table 4.19
Case 1 Results, Nonoverlapped 5X

Known	Average of Raw Scores	Standard Deviation of Raw Scores	Confidence in Best Choice
A	0.276085	0.004147	0.995
B	0.272999	0.022852	0.900
C	0.319048	0.007091	0.999
D	0.291969	0.012976	0.999
E	0.273025	0.006117	0.990
F	**0.256296**	**0.009489**	

Table 4.20
Nonoverlapped 5X, No Speaker A

Known	Average of Raw Scores	Standard Deviation of Raw Scores	Confidence in Best Choice
B	0.269375	0.015905	0.950
C	0.303157	0.016738	0.995
D	0.281192	0.001436	0.999
E	0.266857	0.010649	0.950
F	**0.25384**	**0.00412**	

Table 4.21
Nonoverlapped 5X, No Speaker A With Impostor

Known	Average of Raw Scores	Standard Deviation of Raw Scores	Confidence in Best Choice
B	0.269375	0.015905	0.999
C	0.303157	0.016738	0.999
D	0.281192	0.001436	0.999
E	0.266857	0.010649	0.999
F	0.253838	0.004122	0.999
Impostor #1a	**0.208231**	**0.010277**	

SBI Case 2

In this case, the task was to determine if the male person speaking a bomb threat matched the primary suspect in the case—that is, Type 2 verification. The difficulties in this case were that the unknown recording was short, that training data for the suspect (known) consisted of only one session, and that there was no reference population against which to match.

The strategy used for this case was to determine the intraspeaker variance with cross-validation. Then, a population of reference speakers was created and used for determining the interspeaker variance. Finally, a confidence value for the verification was determined by analyzing the overlap of distributions.

A diagram of the cross-validation strategy is shown in Figure 4.23. The "self-test" arrows in the figure represent comparisons between different segments of the data file for the known speaker. Thus, segment A is compared with B and C, B is compared with C and A, and C is compared with A and B. The average and standard deviation of these tests are shown in Table 4.22 in the row entitled, "Known 3 Separate Segments Against Each Other." The average raw score of these tests gives us an estimate of the intraspeaker variance.

The arrows between the unknown and the segments of the known represent the nonoverlapped cross-validation comparisons between the unknown and the known. Thus, the unknown was compared with segments A, B, and C. The results are also shown in Table 4.22. The interspeaker variance is described by this average distortion value. By comparing the two averages in Table 4.22, we should be able to determine whether or not the unknown differs from the known (interspeaker variance) as much as the known varies with itself (intraspeaker variance). However, the intraspeaker variance is artificially low since the three segments were all recorded at the same time. Therefore, the results in

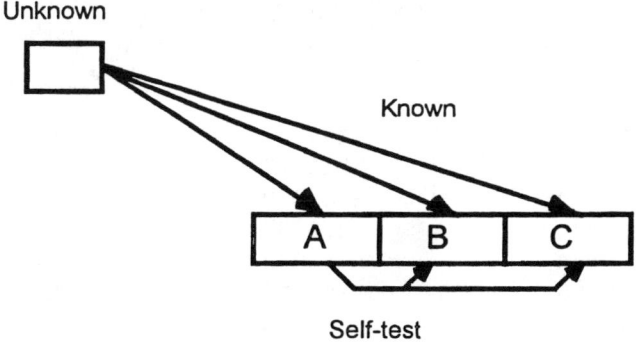

Figure 4.23 Case 2 cross-validation strategy.

Table 4.22
Case 2 Self-Test Results

Test	Average of Raw Scores	Standard Deviation of Raw Scores
Known 3 Separate Segments Against Each Other	0.08759	0.00853
Unknown Against 3 Separate Segments	0.14728	0.00532

Table 4.22 do not support any decision about the identity of the unknown.

A reference population was created from the set of all male speakers in the set of SBI tapes. A model was created for each of these eight impostors. Each of the extracted files for the impostors had a duration approximately equal to the duration of the suspect's file. Then, the model for the unknown was compared with models of the eight impostors and a model of the suspect.

Table 4.23 shows the suspect's recognition scores followed by the impostors' scores. The raw scores are the actual

Table 4.23
Case 2 Impostor Test

Known	Raw	Normalized
Suspect	0.143751	0.973340
Impostor #2a	0.243472	0.470898
Impostor #2b	0.230009	0.578489
Impostor #2c	0.227065	0.601382
Impostor #2d	0.247048	0.442380
Impostor #2e	0.193276	0.825421
Impostor #2f	0.285308	0.180187
Impostor #2g	0.296207	0.128522
Impostor #2h	0.292427	0.145190

distortion values from the recognizer. The normalized scores are the positions of the raw scores on a normal distribution curve.

Since the suspect has a raw score much lower than any of the impostors, the suspect is believed to be the same speaker as the unknown. The normalized score for the suspect is an estimate of the confidence in this decision. Again, the SBI agent informed us that our decision was correct [2].

SBI Case 3

Case 3 was a verification task similar to SBI Case 2, in which the task was to determine if the male speakers on two tapes were the same person. The unknown was recorded using a body-recording device and was of poor quality. The known was recorded in an interrogation room and was of marginal quality. Thus, this task was Type 3, since it had two unknown channels. (It could have been Type 2 if the known had been recorded under better conditions.) Again, exemplars of impostors were taken from other male speakers in the set of SBI tapes.

Table 4.24 shows the results from a test in which the unknown and the suspect are speaking the same sentence and the impostors are saying completely different sentences. Table 4.25 shows the results of a test in which all known speakers speak different sentences. In both tables, the table row corresponding to the suspect is shown in italics.

In both tests, the suspect's score is close to the mean score and therefore is determined unlikely to be the same speaker as the unknown. The decision was confirmed by the SBI agent [2].

By analyzing three of the four possible types of forensic tasks, we have demonstrated the system's ability to solve real forensic cases. Type 4 tasks could not be simulated since we do not currently have a large enough suspect database.

Table 4.24
Case 3, Impostor Test With Key Sentence

Known	Raw	Normalized
Suspect	0.21188	0.67494
Impostor #3a	0.29670	0.21683
Impostor #3b	0.18465	0.80244
Impostor #3c	0.21982	0.63225
Impostor #3d	0.14842	0.91603
Impostor #3e	0.21366	0.66557
Impostor #3f	0.33698	0.08538
Impostor #3g	0.34738	0.06402
Impostor #3h	0.22753	0.58928

Table 4.25
Case 3, Impostor Test With Remainder of Unknown

Known	Raw	Normalized
Suspect	0.23909	0.41332
Impostor #3a	0.25653	0.30208
Impostor #3b	0.15997	0.87252
Impostor #3c	0.17553	0.80830
Impostor #3d	0.18232	0.77486
Impostor #3e	0.18493	0.76134
Impostor #3f	0.29847	0.10792
Impostor #3g	0.32651	0.04279
Impostor #3h	0.21362	0.58636

SUMMARY

In this chapter, we presented the results of experiments that used the voice-recognition system described in Chapter 3. These results show that the system has the potential to be a powerful tool in the demanding sphere of forensics and hence in many other applications as well.

The preliminary experiments provide us with the basis for most of the research described in this monograph. One early experiment demonstrated that the current voice-recognition system could perform accurately on utterances as short as one-fourth of a sentence—less than the duration of a typical voice-crime exemplar.

Other experiments demonstrated the accuracy of the system with large numbers of known speakers. These experiments measure the system's performance with the largest standard database currently available for testing purposes. On the average, the current voice-recognition system is able to eliminate 99.6% of the population from consideration in a population of 230 male speakers. Evidence from tests of other population sizes shows that this level of accuracy should be obtainable with larger populations as well.

Experiments for verifying the effectiveness of channel variation compensation techniques were also described in detail. Preliminary tests on the rehumanizing filter technique showed it to be an effective method for compensating for unknown channels. This technique will permit the use of voice-recognition systems in the noisy environments common in forensic cases.

The possibility of using secondary parameters to improve recognition accuracy was also investigated. Pitch and moment function were as used as secondary parameters.

The current voice-recognition system was tested on mock cases provided by the NCSBI. The system was able to recognize criminals correctly by their voices alone in several mock cases in which the recordings were made using standard law enforcement equipment and procedures. The techniques for using the automated system to determine both a decision and a confidence value for that decision were described in detail.

References

[1] Koster, Barrett E, *Automatic Lip-Sync: Direct Translation of Speech Sound to Mouth Animation*, Ph.D. dissertation, North Carolina State University, Raleigh, NC, March 1995.

[2] Robertson, M. D., North Carolina State Bureau of Investigation, personal communication, 1995.

The Future of Context-Free Voice Recognition

5

In this chapter we will present our view of what lies ahead in the area of context-free voice recognition. As we have done all along, we will focus on the area of forensic applications to make the discussion as concrete as possible.

First, we will indicate directions for further investigating the rehumanizing filter technique. This will help clarify and reinforce our conclusions about this new method for dealing with the unknown-channel problem.

We will then suggest methods for constructing appropriate speaker databases for voice recognition when faced with scenarios of Types 2, 3, or 4 (as discussed in Chapter 3). Next, we will comment on the medium- and long-term goals of voice-recognition research. Finally, we will mention some further applications of context-free voice recognition, especially in forensics.

REHUMANIZING FILTER TECHNIQUE TESTS

In this section, we will propose experiments to verify further the rehumanizing filter technique. Further experiments are needed to show that the technique performs accurately under more life-like conditions.

We tested the rehumanizing filter technique by simulating the filtering caused by a communication channel. To complete the evaluation of the technique, the tester must use real communication channels. A known clean exemplar should be transmitted through a communications channel and recorded at the other end. The devices comprising the channel should be characterized electronically, in terms of the attenuation and phase shift that occur at various frequencies for signals passed through the devices.

At that point, the rehumanizing filter technique may be used to guess the channel as if it were unknown. By performing several experiments of this type, the tester may measure the accuracy of the technique for determining the correct filter to use. The resulting speaker-recognition performance can also be measured.

In the experiments performed so far, the search for the correct filter consisted simply of varying one parameter (filter order or cutoff frequency) until some criterion of the raw distortion score was met—for example, the average standard deviation or the minimum of the scores was minimized. In searching for the correct filter in a real-life situation, new search strategies must be developed, since modeling the real filter by only one or two parameters is not sufficient.

The search space is likely to be ill-defined, containing many peaks and valleys. To prevent the search algorithm from improperly terminating while in a local minimum, an intelligent search strategy is necessary. Some possible choices include neural networks, genetic algorithms, or simulated annealing. In brief, methods of artificial intelligence may need to be exploited.

Once an appropriate strategy has been identified, a fully automated system based on the new strategy should be developed. The new system could be tested by using the TIMIT or other databases and rerecording the unknown exemplars after they have been passed through a known communication channel. Another excellent way to evaluate the system is to use the kind of realistic data furnished us by the NCSBI (as discussed in Chapter 4). Law enforcement agencies have a tremendous interest in voice recognition and, as they were in our case, would likely be willing to assist in any research endeavors.

The rehumanizing filter technique is independent of whatever methods of pattern matching are used during the actual recognition process. Thus, another method for evaluating the technique is to test it with other pattern-matching techniques, including off-the-shelf speaker verification systems.

The rehumanizing filter technique may even be useful for improving the performance of speech-recognition systems whose input may be corrupted by channel passage. First, a voice-recognition system would be used to make the speech "sound more human." Then, the filtered signal could be used as input to a speech-recognition system. This strategy seems feasible to us, though we have not tested it per se. It would be particularly effective in cases in which the speech to be recognized, and the pattern templates against which recognition takes place, came through different channels.

VOICE-RECOGNITION DATABASES

Most of the performance tests described in this book were carried out under controlled conditions. Controllable input conditions are necessary for scientific experiments but do not allow for accurate predictions about recognition performance under real-life conditions. The TIMIT Database, which was used extensively as input to the recognition algorithms, has many desirable properties for performing tests on context-free voice-recognition systems. However, its quality is too good. The TIMIT Database was recorded under the best possible recording conditions and contains only one recording session per speaker. One may compensate for the exceedingly good recording quality by filtering the speech signal digitally or even transmitting signals through actual communication paths that corrupt them. In our research as of this writing, only digital filtering of the signals has been performed to corrupt the speech in a controllable manner. In future experiments, realistic filtering—by transmitting speech signals through, say, a real telephone system—might be tried.

No modifications of the TIMIT Database can compensate for its lack of multiple recording sessions. In the experiments described in this book, the test and training utterances were recorded in the same session. Thus, the recordings did not contain the expected natural variation of speakers' voices. This natural variance is important in voice recognition, especially forensic voice recognition, because recordings of voice crimes and of suspect interrogations would probably not occur on the same day. The lack of natural variance may cause experimental recognition scores to be better than in real life situations.[1] Experiments on noncontemporaneous speech, in which the unknowns are recorded at different times than the knowns, must be performed in the future.

In view of the inability to compensate for the lack of natural variance in the TIMIT Database, other databases must be used. The SPIDRE Database does contain multiple recording sessions per speaker, but it has other drawbacks that prohibit its use for testing voice-recognition systems. The main problem is that each of the four conversations per speaker is recorded on a different unknown channel. Thus, a reference to what the speaker actually sounds like is unob-

---

1. The combined experience of the authors bears this assertion out. As documented in [1], there appear to be five levels of speech-processing systems. The best performance takes place in the experimenter's laboratory using idealized data. Performance declines in the lab when more realistic data are used. When the system goes "into the field" to be tested on ideal data, its performance is worse than in the lab and worsens further when realistic data are introduced. Finally, when the system is put into actual operation on actual data, its performance is worst of all. This seemingly cynical view has been borne out numerous times in the history of speech processing. Most descriptions of performance, especially when they come from vendors of the speech-processing system, report Level One results—in the lab with idealized data. In this book, we have reported on Levels One and Two.

tainable. Only Type 3 tasks can be simulated with the SPIDRE Database.

Many other voice databases are available through the Linguistic Data Consortium (LDC; see Chapter 2, footnote 2). However, none have the qualities most needed for research in forensic voice recognition. A database for testing such a system should contain input data in a format suitable for addressing the four types of forensic cases we have defined. A database specifically designed for research on forensic voice recognition should contain multiple recording sessions for a variety of speakers. The set of speakers should contain subsets of similar-sounding speakers—for example, sharing the same sex, age, and dialect—to make the voice-recognition task realistic.

For training the known speakers, several sessions of clean recordings are necessary. Each training session should contain at least 30 seconds of net speech. The recording sessions should be separated by at least one week. In the training sessions, the text should be as free as possible—that is, anything can be said, and the speakers should use their normal conversational voice. Transcriptions of the conversations would not be necessary.

For testing the unknown speakers, several examples of "voice crimes" should be recorded per speaker. These exemplars should have durations equal to typical voice crimes. However, the set of unknown speakers does not have to be as large as the set of known speakers. For each exemplar, there should be several versions: a cleanly recorded version and versions transmitted via various channels—for example, public and private telephones, personal answering machines, body recorders, and 911 logging devices. Variations on the speaking style or mood of speaker would also be useful. For example, the set of exemplars for a speaker might contain recordings in a normal conversational voice, an angry voice, and several intentionally disguised voices. Again, transcriptions of the conversations would not be necessary; however, information about the speaker, the speaking style, and channel would be required.

With access to a database similar to the one described above, researchers would be able to test forensic voice-recognition systems in a realistic manner. If a standard database could be agreed upon, the relative performance of two forensic voice-recognition systems could be compared fairly. Similar testing procedures have been implemented in other areas of computer speech research, such as speech recognition. The database could be stored on a collection of CD-ROM discs and distributed through the LDC.

MEDIUM-TERM GOALS

In this section, we will discuss medium-term goals in voice recognition. These goals include tasks that could be realistically completed within one to two years.

First, the effect of disguises must be addressed. To form a rough estimate, recognition rates for different disguise techniques, such as raised pitch, lowered pitch, increased nasality, and dialect change, should be examined. Recognition scores are likely to be worse than in the ideal case, but the experiment should be able to determine the extent of performance degradation. A more intensive study of disguises should reveal how the speech waveforms are changed. If the disguise technique itself can be identified in an exemplar, then it may be possible to compensate for it.

A second goal for the not-too-distant future is to coordinate research efforts in forensic voice recognition with law enforcement agencies and the offices of attorneys-general or the appropriate arm of justice departments. Researchers should visit law enforcement facilities and meet with agents to determine the requirements of forensic voice-recognition systems and protocols for using them.

Researchers should try to persuade law enforcement agencies to follow the procedures given in Chapter 3 for collecting data from suspects. These procedures must also be refined as more information is made available.

LONG-TERM GOALS

This section will discuss any relevant research endeavor not fulfillable within two years. First, to create an *ideal* speaker recognition system as described in Chapter 3, finding a correlation between parameters of a speech waveform and the physical measurements of the vocal tract that created the waveform is highly desirable. A brute-force strategy for determining such a correlation would be to use automated learning techniques, such as neural networks, to look for correlations in sets of data. Care must be taken not to allow the system to over-train and return coincidental correlations as real correlations.

For a brute-force strategy to succeed, large quantities of data must be available. Therefore, a large number of speakers would have to be recorded and have the dimensions of their vocal tracts physically measured. The physical measurements could be made from radiographs or magnetic resonance imaging (MRI) images. The major problem with this approach is the cost and time involved, but it may be the only strategy for achieving the highest possible recognition rates.

Another long-term goal is the creation of a database for testing forensic voice-recognition systems. However, to perform any research prior to the construction of such a database, a smaller-scaled version would be necessary. Creating a real forensic database, in the manner described earlier in this chapter, would be a time-consuming endeavor requiring expensive equipment, trained personnel, and an extensive subject population willing to have their voices recorded.

In addition to developing a database for specifically testing systems, a database of reference impostors and suspects is needed if the systems are to be put to regular use by law enforcement agencies when voice crimes are committed. The amount of data per speaker in the reference/suspect database (RSDB) would be considerably smaller than in the databases for testing since interest would be focused on the speaker him/herself rather than on system-testing. For example, 30 seconds of speech per person would be plenty for the RSDB, but for testing a system we would want many minutes of speech per person to keep the size of the subject population manageable.

The RSDB would be similar to existing and planned fin-gerprint, photograph, and DNA-sample databases. An RSDB might take decades to create if the goal is to get recordings of all speakers in the country. Similar to the strategy for collecting DNA samples, the first step toward building a state-wide or nationwide RSDB would be to get exemplars from known criminals.

One problem with this database is that voices, unlike fingerprints and DNA samples, change over time. However, it seems possible that the effects of aging could be compensated for in a manner similar to compensation for disguises. The "aging" of recorded voices is a vital and fascinating area of future research.

When the size of the RSDB exceeds a certain level, new techniques for effectively searching the database will be required. First, multikey lookups would be necessary to limit the search space only to speakers of similar age, sex, and dialect. However, these sets of speakers will still be very large; thus, determining the distortion between the unknown and every member of a reduced search space may still be impractical. Thus, methods for further reducing search space will be necessary.

OTHER APPLICATIONS

Thus far, the application of voice recognition for forensic use has been limited to the problem of identifying criminals. Another application of this technology is verifying that a known criminal is at a certain place, say by answering a specific telephone.

To reduce prison overcrowding, some less dangerous convicts are placed under "house arrest." The criminal is forced by law to stay in his or her own house. Currently, house arrest is enforced by electronic devices attached to the prisoners' bodies. The devices are expensive and can be disabled or otherwise fooled.

Voice-recognition technology could be used to assist in solving this problem. At random intervals, a computer system could call the prisoner's home telephone. After greeting the convict, the automated system would record samples of the convict's speech. If the new recordings correctly matched previous recordings of the prisoner, the prisoner could be left alone and trusted at least until the next call. However, if the telephone were not answered, or the voice that answered the phone did not match the prisoner's voice, then prison officials could investigate further.

In this application, an error is much less costly than the error of false conviction or innocence, so the voice-recognition system need not meet the rigorous specifications required in the investigative and judicial arenas. The system would be cost-effective, we think, though this is another area that needs research. A fully automated system would require little maintenance. The only personnel needed after the system was installed would be the law enforcement agents needed to check on those inmates who had either been subject to false-rejection errors or had actually fled their residences. Since such a system appears to offer many more benefits than liabilities, we recommend that a feasibility study be carried out in the near future.

SUMMARY

In this chapter, we have reviewed several ideas for future research in forensic voice recognition. These ideas include experiments for further testing the rehumanizing filter technique as well as long-term goals for alternative forensic applications of voice-recognition technology.

References

[1] Biermann, A.W., Rodman, R., et al, "Interactive Natural Language Problem Solving: A Pragmatic Approach," *Proceedings of the Conference on Applied Natural Language Processing,* Association for Computational Linguistics and the Naval Research Laboratory, 1983, pp. 180–191.

Conclusions 6

In this book, we have discussed new techniques intended to advance the state of the art of voice recognition. To provide the reader with a frame of reference, we first defined the fundamental concepts of voice recognition, such as the difference between text-dependent and text-independent (context-free) voice recognition or between speaker identification and speaker verification.

In Chapter 2, we presented a history of voice-recognition achievements, starting with the voiceprints of the 1960s and spanning the decades to 1997. This history includes our own endeavors using segregating systems.

Our research in voice recognition was targeted at the forensic and judicial arenas. We chose these areas because they are the most challenging of all voice-recognition applications; the population size may be unlimited, the channel may be unknown, the content of the utterance is entirely unconstrained, and the speakers are uncooperative. Thus, solutions to forensic voice-recognition problems will most likely encompass other voice-recognition applications. Many of the new techniques described in this book will be useful for improving any voice-recognition system.

The book makes several specific contributions toward the goal of ideal forensic voice recognition. The first of these is a taxonomy of forensic voice-recognition tasks. This taxonomy is important for describing the inherent difficulties and differences of each task. It is much more descriptive than the "identification versus verification" classification used by researchers in the past.

The second major contribution is a description of the structure and expectations of ideal voice-recognition systems. This discussion was motivated by the need to determine a theoretical upper bound on performance. It was determined that an ideal system must base recognition decisions on parameters that are directly related to the physical dimensions of speakers' vocal tracts. By correlating parameters to physical measurements, the recognition system could avoid being deceived by impostors intentionally trying to sound like another person. Two techniques for creating an ideal system were discussed: derived physical parameter-based and set/constraint-based. The investigation of the structure of ideal voice-recognition systems revealed several insights into ways to build better, though not quite ideal, systems.

A new voice-recognition system was constructed based on these insights. The details of this system were described in Chapter 3. The system used a segregating approach, but a change in the segregation step was implemented to allow the system to find local areas of the parameter space in which each speaker was unique. Specifically, coarse resolution parameters were used for segregation and fine resolution parameters were used for classification. The new system also includes a novel distance measure that normalizes the distortion at each point in the frequency spectrum by the energy at that frequency. This normalization reduces the effects of formant peak variation. Furthermore, the new system contains methods for dealing with the absence of information that occurs when a speaker's model contains no vectors in a certain category.

Another contribution to the advancement of voice-recognition performance is the rehumanizing filter technique. Channel variance is one the most significant problems impeding the performance of voice-recognition systems. The channel variance problem is analogous to an algebraic problem with one equation (the exemplar of the known speaker) and two unknown variables (the identity of the speaker and characteristics of the channel). The only information that investigators have is the fact that the voice is human. The rehumanizing filter technique exploits this single kernel of knowledge by attempting to determine an inverse filter to compensate for the unknown channel's filter characteristics. The parameters of the inverse filter are varied until the unknown speaker sounds most human-like. The new technique is a major step towards conquering an all-but-insoluble problem.

A fourth contribution of this work is the definition of a set of protocols for the use of voice-recognition systems in forensic settings. These procedures include recommendations for the collection of data, the use of cross-validation, and the presentation of results. To compare the relative performance of forensic voice-recognition systems, a new metric, APE, was developed.

In Chapter 4, the results of many voice-recognition experiments were presented, accompanied by various graphs, charts, tables, pictures, and diagrams. Some of the experiments were simply conventional performance tests of the new voice-recognition system. Others were intended to test voice-recognition systems on tasks that had not previously been scientifically tested.

For example, most data reported in the literature concerns experiments with small populations of known speakers. Our system testing used the entire male and female populations of the TIMIT Database (290 and 130 speakers, respectively). Both these population sizes are large compared with those of other published experiments.

We also presented the first summary of experiments performed on input data that had actually been recorded using standard law enforcement recording devices, such as body recorders, 911 logging devices, and answering machines.

Finally, in Chapter 5, we gave an outline of the future research required to advance the state of the art in forensic voice recognition. This outline was intended to point out the areas most in need of immediate attention, broken down as medium- and long-term goals. The chapter also includes a description of experiments required to verify further the voice-recognition innovations proposed in this book.

In summary, we have created the foundation for a substantial research and development program in the area of forensic voice recognition. A laboratory version of a system was created and is ready to be tested on actual forensic cases.

In addition to providing readers with more insight about the nature of speech production and the uniqueness of the human voice, this research program has the potential to affect the general population as well. The security of public buildings, certainly a relevant issue in today's society, can be improved through voice-recognition technology. In the near future, we expect to be able to meet the judicial criteria for convicting voice criminals such as persons who leave bomb threats. Already, the use of voice-recognition systems for narrowing the search of suspects is feasible. Even the deterrent value of having such a system available to law enforcement agencies would be a valuable asset.

The improved quality of life that forensic voice-recognition systems bring to society is powerful enough justification for us to carry out the research and for interested parties to read this book.

About the Authors

Dr. Richard L. Klevans is currently a research associate in the Department of Computer Science at North Carolina State University. He received his doctoral degree and his masters from North Carolina State in 1995 and 1991, respectively. His current research interests include network-based education and speech processing.

Dr. Robert D. Rodman earned a masters degree in mathematics and a Ph.D. in linguistics at UCLA. He is currently on the faculty of the Computer Science Department at North Carolina State University. He was previously on the faculty of the University of North Carolina at Chapel Hill, and prior to that he worked for General Electric Company, Burroughs Corporation, and IBM. He has been publishing since 1963. His works include books on linguistics and speech processing.

Index

Absence of evidence problem, 91
Absorbing state, 41
Acoustic segment unit, 44
Activation function, 45–46
Additive noise, 55–56, 94, 115
Age, speaker, 65, 67, 158
ANN. *See* Neural networks, artificial
APE metric. *See* Average percent eliminated metric
ASU. *See* Acoustic segment unit
AT&T Bell Laboratories, 2–3
Attenuation, spectral region, 56
Autocorrelation function, 77–79
Average filter compensation, 95–97, 117–19, 122–24
Average percent eliminated metric, 104, 112–13, 118, 121
Average spectrum, utterance, 95–96
Averaging channel characteristics, 56

Bandpass filtering, 21, 55, 94–95
    average filter compensation, 95–97
    rehumanizing filter, 97–99
Bar voiceprint, 16
    See also Speech spectogram
Bayesian classifier, 74
Bell, Alexander Graham, 2, 3
Binary neural network, 50–51
Binary tree search, 50–51, 91–94
Bolt, Richard, 17–18
Butterworth filter, 118–19

Centroid, generic codebook, 82–83, 85–86
Cepstral coefficient, 24, 26, 30–31, 35, 52, 55–56, 67, 75
Cepstrum, 24

Channel characterization, 55–56
Channel compensation tests, 116–17
    average filter, 117–19
    rehumanizing filter, 119–21
Channel mismatch, 118–19
Channel variation, 8–9, 35, 55, 94–95, 162–63
    average filter, 95–96
    rehumanizing filter, 97–99
Clipped autocorrelation coefficient, 55
Closed-set identification, 9, 34–35, 62, 91
Coarse resolution parameter, 73–75
Cocktail party effect, 4
Codebook, vector quantization, 36–38, 43, 52–53, 82–86, 109, 114–15
Comparison, feature vectors, 87–91, 115
Comparison, two speakers, 130–31
Computer systems security, 6
Conditioning, digital signal, 21
Constraints systems, 68–71
Context-free voice recognition. *See* Text-independent voice recognition
Continuous hidden Markov model, 42, 44
Continuous-speech voice recognition, 53
Contour voiceprint, 16
Cross-validation, 137–47
Cutoff parameter, 131–32

Databases
    reference suspects, 157–58
    search techniques, 158
    system testing, 32–33, 157
    usage factors, 153–56
Data reduction, 54
Decision names, 133
Delta-Cepstrum coefficient, 26

Delta-type features, 55
Digital computer hardware, 20
Digital filtering, 153
Digital signal processing, 20–21, 66–71
Discrete hidden Markov model, 42
Discrete-word speech recognition, 8
Discriminator counting, 54
Disguises, voice, 65–66, 156
Distance measures
 Euclidean, 24, 29–30, 35, 85
 Manhattan, 30
 principles, 29–31
 segregating systems, 52
 vector comparison, 75, 89
Distortion values
 secondary features, 128–30
 speaker comparison, 87–93
Double-hidden-layer neural network, 49
DSP. *See* Digital signal processing
Dynamic time warping, 3, 53

Edge effects, 79
Emotional state, speaker, 65
Ergotic hidden Markov model, 40–41, 43–44, 52–53, 74
Error back-propagation training, 48–49
Error rates
 factors affecting, 32, 54
 hidden Markov model, 43–44
 long-term averaging, 35
 neural network, 49, 51
 noise effects, 54–55
 segregating system, 93–94
 utterance length, 110–11
 vector quantization, 38
Euclidean, 30
Euclidean distance measure, 24, 29–30, 35, 85
Evidence, absence of, 91
Extraction. *See* Feature extraction

False acceptance, 35, 93
False rejection, 35, 93, 159
Fast Fourier transform, 22–23, 76, 89, 100, 108, 124
FBI. *See* Federal Bureau of Investigation
Feature effectiveness criterion, 28
Feature extraction
 defined, 15
 digital signal processing, 66–68
 evaluation process, 27–29
 ideal systems, 66–71
 parameter types, 21–27
 physical features, 65–68
 process, 20–21, 84
 segregating system, 76–82
 sound ranges, 68–71
 utterance length, 108–9
Features, secondary, 121, 124–31
 cutoff value, 131–32
 moment values, 121, 124–26
 pitch, 121, 130
 standard deviation, 125–30
 usage, 130–35
Feature vector segregation, 82–87
FEC. *See* Feature effectiveness criterion
Federal Bureau of Investigation, 19
Feedforward neural network, 47–49
Feedforward recall, 48
FFT. *See* Fast Fourier transform
Filter order, 120
Filtered data test, 114–16
Filtering, 26, 79
 signal degradation, 116–17
 speech corruption, 153–54
 See also Bandpass filtering
Fine resolution parameter, 73–75
Fingerprint, 16
Finite duration impulse response, 25
FIR. *See* Finite duration impulse response
Floating point value, 87
Forensic recognition classification, 75, 97, 99
 APE metric, 104
 applications, 158–59
 cross-validation, 137–144
 databases for, 104–5, 157
 law enforcement coordination, 156–57
 logistics, 101–105
 mock cases, 135–48
 speech variation factor, 154
 suspects, known/unknown, 62–64
 test utterance length, 107
Formant frequencies, 17, 23, 55, 66, 75, 80, 82, 86, 108
Formant peaks, 89
Fourier Bessel functions, 54
Frame, time-delayed neural network, 51
F-ratio, 27–28, 31, 34
Frequency representation, 22–23
Fundamental frequency, 55
Fuzzy set recognition, 68–74

Gaussian mixture model, 54
Gaussian probability distribution function, 56
Global areas of uniqueness, 72

Global soft-decision search, 50
GPDF. *See* Gaussian probability distribution function

Hamming function, 79–82
Harmonics, lower, 115, 119
Heisenberg Uncertainty Principle, 23
Hidden Markov models, 3
  circular, 42, 43
  left-to-right, 41–43
  preprocessing, 45
  problems, 41–42
  segregating system, 52–53, 74–75
  text-dependent system, 42–43, 45
  text-independent system, 43–45
HMM. *See* Hidden Markov models

Ideal voice-recognition system, 64–71, 157
IDS. *See* Intensity deviation spectrum
Imposters, 17
Impulse response function, 25
Integer value, 87
Integrated circuit, 2
Intensity deviation spectrum, 26
Interspeaker variance, 17, 145
Intraspeaker variance, 17, 35, 144–47, 154
Inverse filter, 98–99, 163
Inverse filter spectral coefficient, 23, 35, 74–75, 80, 83, 86, 108

Jaw position values, 126

Kempelen, Wolfgang von, 2
Kersta, L.G., 17–18
King database, 33
K-nearest neighbor, 54
Koenig, Bruce, 19
Koster's jaw position parameter, 121, 124
Kratzenstein, Christian Gottlieb, 1–2

Language identification, 4
Law enforcement, 6–8
  agency coordination, 156–57
  Federal Bureau of Investigation, 19
  forensic recognition, 62–64
  text-independent systems, 61–64
  See also Forensic recognition classification
LDC. *See* Linguistic Data Consortium
Learning rate, 48
LGB algorithm. *See* Linde, Gray, and Buzo algorithm
Liftering, 56
Linde, Gray, and Buzo algorithm, 82

Linear predictive coding, 23–25, 30, 52, 66, 75, 80, 82, 108
Line spectral pair, 26
Linguistic Data Consortium, 155–56
Lip synching, 5
Local areas of uniqueness, 72–73
Log area coefficient, 25
Long-term averaging, 34–36
LPC. *See* Linear predictive coding
LSP. *See* Line spectral pair

Magnetic resonance imaging, 157
Manhattan distance measure, 30
Moment values, 121, 125–27
Motorola 56001, 100
MRI. *See* Magnetic resonance imaging
Multilayer feedforward neural network, 47–48

NCSBI. *See* North Carolina State Bureau of Investigation
Net speech, 102
Neural networks, artificial, 3
  activation function, 45–46
  binary tree search, 50–51
  characteristics, 45, 71
  data correlation, 157
  global soft-decision search, 50
  multilayer feedforward, 47–48
  time-delayed, 51
  training, 48
  voice recognition, 49–50
Neurons, 45
NN. *See* Neural networks, artificial
Nodes, 45
Noisy environments, 54–56, 65
Noncontemporaneous speech, 154
Normalization
  recognition scores, 92–93
  vector comparison, 89
North Carolina State Bureau of Investigation, 62, 135, 152

Off-line operation, 9
Open-set identification, 9
Orthogonalization, 53

Parameter extraction. *See* Feature extraction
Parameters, secondary. *See* Features, secondary
PARCOR. *See* Partial correlation coefficient
Partial correlation coefficient, 26
Passwords, security, 6

Pattern recognition
  defined, 15
  hidden Markov model, 38–45
  long-term averaging, 34–35
  miscellaneous techniques, 53–54
  neural network, 45–51
  segregating system, 51–53
  training/testing, 32–33
  vector quantization, 36–38
Perceptron, 45
Perceptual linear predictive, 26, 55
Personal identification number, 6
Phase distortion, 55, 94
Phone-like unit, 44
Physical features parameters, 66–68
Physical state, speaker, 65, 67
Pitch, 21–22, 35, 55, 66–67, 121, 130
Pitch peak, 76, 78–79, 95
PLP. See Perceptual linear predictive
PLU. See Phone-like unit
Population size, 112–13
Preemphasis, 79–82
Preprocessing
  digital signal, 20–21
  hidden Markov model, 45
  noise separation, 55
Probabilistic acoustic map, 54
Probability density function, 54
Prosodics, 2–3
Pseudoknown segment, 137–38
Pseudounknown segment, 137–38

RASTA. See Relative spectral-based coefficient
Real-time operation, 9
Recognition, hidden Markov model, 41
Recording environment, ideal versus noisy, 8–9
Recording sessions, multiple, 154–55
Reference/suspect database, 157–58
Reflection coefficient, 24
Rehumanizing filter technique, 97–99, 119–21, 125, 151–53, 163
Relative spectral-based coefficient, 26, 55
Relative spectral perceptual linear predictive, 55
RSDB. See Reference/suspect database

SDWD. See Smoothed discrete Wigner distribution
Security systems, voice-based, 6–7
Segregating voice-recognition systems
  channel variation, 94–99
  concepts, 72–75
  feature extraction, 76–82
  principles, 51–53, 109
  recognition decisions, 91–94
  software implementation, 99–101
  vector comparison, 87–91
  vector segregation, 45, 82–87
Sequence, hidden Markov model, 41
Short-file outlier, 140
Sigmoidal activation function, 45–46
Signal-to-noise ratio, 55, 75
Single-hidden-layer neural network, 49
Smoothed discrete Wigner distribution, 26
SNR. See Signal-to-noise ratio
Software, 99–101
Soong, F.K., 38
Sound ranges, for modeling speakers, 68–71
Sound spectograph, 17
Speaker classification, 4–6
Speaker identification
  defined, 9
  neural network, 49–50
Speaker recognition. See Voice recognition
Speaker separation, 4
Speaker variance. See Variance, interspeaker and intraspeaker
Speaker verification
  defined, 9
  neural network, 49
Spectogram. See Speech spectogram
Spectral coefficient, 23, 35, 74–75, 80, 83, 86, 108
Spectral flattening, 21
Spectral moment, 67
Speech processing. See Speaker classification; Speaker identification; Speaker verification; Speech synthesis; Voice recognition
Speech recognition. See Voice recognition
Speech spectogram, 16, 19
Speech synthesis, 1–3
SPIDRE database, 33, 154–55
Standard deviation, secondary features, 125–29
STD. See Standard deviation, secondary features
Subword unit model, 44–45

TDNN. See Time-delayed neural network
Telephone call tracing, 97–98
Template, vector quantization, 37

Testing, voice recognition, 7, 32–33
    hidden Markov model, 44
    speaker modeling time, 71
    unknown speaker, 155
Text-dependent voice recognition, 7–8, 26
    channel characterization, 55–56
    hidden Markov model, 42–43
    subword unit model, 45
    utterance unit model, 45
    vector quantization, 37–38
Text-independent voice recognition, 7–8, 12
    features used, 25–26
    hidden Markov model, 43–44
    ideal systems, 64–71
    law enforcement use, 61–64
    long-term averaging, 35
    segregating system, 51
    subword unit model, 45
    utterance unit model, 45
    vector quantization, 37
    See also Segregating voice-recognition systems
Threshold, speaker comparison, 130–31
Threshold cutoff, vector comparison, 90
Time alignment, 38
Time-delayed neural network, 51
TIMIT database, 33, 51, 78, 107, 112–13, 117–21, 153–54, 163
Toeplitz autocorrelation matrix, 30
Training, voice recognition, 7–8, 32–33
    forensic recognition, 64
    hidden Markov model, 41–42, 44
    known speaker, 155
    neural network, 45, 48–49
    segregating system, 82–83
    speaker modeling time, 71
Trajectory space comparison, 54
True average spectrum, 95

Uniqueness, global areas of, 72

Uniqueness, local areas of, 72–73
Unvoiced segment, speech, 76–78, 80
Utterance length, 35, 107–11
Utterance unit model, 44–45
Utterance variation, 26, 65, 71

Variance, interspeaker and intraspeaker, 17, 35
    cross-validation test, 144–47
    importance of, 154
Vector quantization, 36–38
    feature segregation, 52–53, 74–75, 83
    principles, 69
Vocal tract, 6, 23
    measurement, 157
    muscle control, 65–66
    physical parameters, 65–71
Vocoder, 2
Voice coder. *See* Vocoder
Voiced segment, speech, 76–77, 79, 85
Voiceprint analysis
    error rates, 17–19
    principles, 16–20
Voice recognition
    applications, 6–7
    history, 3–4
    principles, 5
Voice signal degradation, 116–17
VQ. *See* Vector quantization

Weighting functions
    autocorrelation, 77–79
    distance measure, 31
    vector comparison, 87–91
Windowing, 79–82

YOHO database, 33

Zero crossing rate, 76–77

The Artech House Telecommunications Library

Vinton G. Cerf, *Series Editor*

Access Networks: Technology and V5 Interfacing, Alex Gillespie

Advanced High-Frequency Radio Communications, Eric E. Johnson, Robert I. Desourdis, Jr., et al.

Advanced Technology for Road Transport: IVHS and ATT, Ian Catling, editor

Advances in Computer Systems Security, Vol. 3, Rein Turn, editor

Advances in Telecommunications Networks, William S. Lee and Derrick C. Brown

Advances in Transport Network Technologies: Photonics Networks, ATM, and SDH, Ken-ichi Sato

An Introduction to International Telecommunications Law, Charles H. Kennedy and M. Veronica Pastor

Asynchronous Transfer Mode Networks: Performance Issues, Second Edition, Raif O. Onvural

ATM Switches, Edwin R. Coover

ATM Switching Systems, Thomas M. Chen and Stephen S. Liu

Broadband: Business Services, Technologies, and Strategic Impact, David Wright

Broadband Network Analysis and Design, Daniel Minoli

Broadband Telecommunications Technology, Byeong Lee, Minho Kang and Jonghee Lee

Cellular Mobile Systems Engineering, Saleh Faruque

Cellular Radio: Analog and Digital Systems, Asha Mehrotra

Cellular Radio: Performance Engineering, Asha Mehrotra

Cellular Radio Systems, D. M. Balston and R. C. V. Macario, editors

CDMA for Wireless Personal Communications, Ramjee Prasad

Client/Server Computing: Architecture, Applications, and Distributed Systems Management, Bruce Elbert and Bobby Martyna

Communication and Computing for Distributed Multimedia Systems, Guojun Lu

Community Networks: Lessons from Blacksburg, Virginia, Andrew Cohill and Andrea Kavanaugh, editors

Computer Networks: Architecture, Protocols, and Software, John Y. Hsu

Computer Mediated Communications: Multimedia Applications, Rob Walters

Computer Telephone Integration, Rob Walters

Convolutional Coding: Fundamentals and Applications, Charles Lee

Corporate Networks: The Strategic Use of Telecommunications, Thomas Valovic

The Definitive Guide to Business Resumption Planning, Leo A. Wrobel

Digital Beamforming in Wireless Communications, John Litva and Titus Kwok-Yeung Lo

Digital Cellular Radio, George Calhoun

Digital Hardware Testing: Transistor-Level Fault Modeling and Testing, Rochit Rajsuman, editor

Digital Switching Control Architectures, Giuseppe Fantauzzi

Digital Video Communications, Martyn J. Riley and Iain E. G. Richardson

Distributed Multimedia Through Broadband Communications Services, Daniel Minoli and Robert Keinath

Distance Learning Technology and Applications, Daniel Minoli

EDI Security, Control, and Audit, Albert J. Marcella and Sally Chen

Electronic Mail, Jacob Palme

Enterprise Networking: Fractional T1 to SONET, Frame Relay to BISDN, Daniel Minoli

Expert Systems Applications in Integrated Network Management, E. C. Ericson, L. T. Ericson, and D. Minoli, editors

FAX: Digital Facsimile Technology and Applications, Second Edition, Dennis Bodson, Kenneth McConnell, and Richard Schaphorst

FDDI and FDDI-II: Architecture, Protocols, and Performance, Bernhard Albert and Anura P. Jayasumana

Fiber Network Service Survivability, Tsong-Ho Wu

Future Codes: Essays in Advanced Computer Technology and the Law, Curtis E. A. Karnow

Guide to Telecommunications Transmission Systems, Anton A. Huurdeman

A Guide to the TCP/IP Protocol Suite, Floyd Wilder

Implementing EDI, Mike Hendry

Implementing X.400 and X.500: The PP and QUIPU Systems, Steve Kille

Inbound Call Centers: Design, Implementation, and Management, Robert A. Gable

Information Superhighways Revisited: The Economics of Multimedia, Bruce Egan

Integrated Broadband Networks, Amit Bhargava

International Telecommunications Management, Bruce R. Elbert

International Telecommunication Standards Organizations, Andrew Macpherson

Internetworking LANs: Operation, Design, and Management, Robert Davidson and Nathan Muller

Introduction to Document Image Processing Techniques, Ronald G. Matteson

Introduction to Error-Correcting Codes, Michael Purser

An Introduction to GSM, Siegmund Redl, Matthias K. Weber and Malcom W. Oliphant

Introduction to Radio Propagation for Fixed and Mobile Communications, John Doble

Introduction to Satellite Communication, Bruce R. Elbert

Introduction to T1/T3 Networking, Regis J. (Bud) Bates

Introduction to Telephones and Telephone Systems, Second Edition, A. Michael Noll

Introduction to X.400, Cemil Betanov

LAN, ATM, and LAN Emulation Technologies, Daniel Minoli and Anthony Alles

Land-Mobile Radio System Engineering, Garry C. Hess

LAN/WAN Optimization Techniques, Harrell Van Norman

LANs to WANs: Network Management in the 1990s, Nathan J. Muller and Robert P. Davidson

Minimum Risk Strategy for Acquiring Communications Equipment and Services, Nathan J. Muller

Mobile Antenna Systems Handbook, Kyohei Fujimoto and J. R. James, editors

Mobile Communications in the U.S. and Europe: Regulation, Technology, and Markets, Michael Paetsch

Mobile Data Communications Systems, Peter Wong and David Britland

Mobile Information Systems, John Walker

Networking Strategies for Information Technology, Bruce Elbert

Packet Switching Evolution from Narrowband to Broadband ISDN, M. Smouts

Packet Video: Modeling and Signal Processing, Naohisa Ohta

Personal Communication Networks: Practical Implementation, Alan Hadden

Personal Communication Systems and Technologies, John Gardiner and Barry West, editors

Practical Computer Network Security, Mike Hendry

Principles of Secure Communication Systems, Second Edition, Don J. Torrieri

Principles of Signaling for Cell Relay and Frame Relay, Daniel Minoli and George Dobrowski

Principles of Signals and Systems: Deterministic Signals, B. Picinbono

Private Telecommunication Networks, Bruce Elbert

Radio-Relay Systems, Anton A. Huurdeman

RF and Microwave Circuit Design for Wireless Communications, Lawrence E. Larson

The Satellite Communication Applications Handbook, Bruce R. Elbert

Secure Data Networking, Michael Purser

Service Management in Computing and Telecommunications, Richard Hallows

Smart Cards, José Manuel Otón and José Luis Zoreda

Smart Card Security and Applications, Mike Hendry

Smart Highways, Smart Cars, Richard Whelan

Successful Business Strategies Using Telecommunications Services, Martin F. Bartholomew

Super-High-Definition Images: Beyond HDTV, Naohisa Ohta, et al.

Television Technology: Fundamentals and Future Prospects, A. Michael Noll

Telecommunications Technology Handbook, Daniel Minoli

Telecommuting, Osman Eldib and Daniel Minoli

Telemetry Systems Design, Frank Carden

Teletraffic Technologies in ATM Networks, Hiroshi Saito

Toll-Free Services: A Complete Guide to Design, Implementation, and Management, Robert A. Gable

Transmission Networking: SONET and the SDH, Mike Sexton and Andy Reid

Troposcatter Radio Links, G. Roda

Understanding Emerging Network Services, Pricing, and Regulation, Leo A. Wrobel and Eddie M. Pope

Understanding GPS: Principles and Applications, Elliot D. Kaplan, editor

Understanding Networking Technology: Concepts, Terms and Trends, Mark Norris

UNIX Internetworking, Second Edition, Uday O. Pabrai

Videoconferencing and Videotelephony: Technology and Standards, Richard Schaphorst

Voice Recognition, Richard L. Klevans and Robert D. Rodman

Wireless Access and the Local Telephone Network, George Calhoun

Wireless Communications in Developing Countries: Cellular and Satellite Systems, Rachael E. Schwartz

Wireless Communications for Intelligent Transportation Systems, Scott D. Elliot and Daniel J. Dailey

Wireless Data Networking, Nathan J. Muller

Wireless LAN Systems, A. Santamaría and F. J. López-Hernández

Wireless: The Revolution in Personal Telecommunications, Ira Brodsky

Writing Disaster Recovery Plans for Telecommunications Networks and LANs, Leo A. Wrobel

X Window System User's Guide, Uday O. Pabrai

For further information on these and other Artech House titles, contact:

Artech House
685 Canton Street
Norwood, MA 02062
781-769-9750
Fax: 781-769-6334
Telex: 951-659
email: artech@artech-house.com

Artech House
Portland House, Stag Place
London SW1E 5XA England
+44 (0) 171-973-8077
Fax: +44 (0) 171-630-0166
Telex: 951-659
email: artech-uk@artech-house.com

WWW: http://www.artech-house.com